DECISION DYNAMICS

Navigate Complexity, Solve Problems, Cultivate Impact, and Empower Leadership through Strategy

DILIP PATIL

Copyright © 2024 by Dilip Patil

All rights reserved. No part of this book may be reproduced in any form without permission in writing from the author.

No part of this publication may be reproduced or transmitted in any form or by any means, mechanical or electronic, including photocopying or recording, information storage and retrieval system, email, or any other means, without permission in writing from the author.

DEDICATION

This book is lovingly dedicated to my family—my unwavering foundation and guiding light. Your endless support and belief in me have fueled my journey of personal growth and have been the cornerstone in bringing this book to life. Your influence resonates in every word written and every lesson shared. Thank you for being my inspiration, my strength, and my home.

YOUR GIFT: "THE SUCCESS FORMULA"

Thank you for joining me with **Decision Dynamics."** As a token of appreciation, I'm excited to offer you a complimentary copy of my eBook, "The Success Formula." This guide has insights and strategies to propel you further on your path to success.

"The Success Formula" complements the principles explored in "Decision Dynamics," providing actionable steps for achieving goals and enhancing one's life. To download your free copy, click the link below or scan the QR code:

This eBook is my way of saying thank you and supporting you in your journey toward success and happiness.

Best wishes,

Dilip Patil

WELCOME TO YOUR LEADERSHIP JOURNEY

"Great leaders are not defined by the absence of weakness, but rather by the presence of clear strengths." —John Zenger.

Thank you for your trust and eagerness to continue this transformative journey with me. If you have journeyed through "Leadership Awakening," "Visionary Pathways," and "Masterful Communication," I am sincerely grateful for your commitment and enthusiastic participation. These books, which form the foundation of the **"LEADERSHIP TRANSFORMED"** series, were just the beginning of our exploration into the multifaceted nature of leadership.

"Decision Dynamics" is designed to build upon this foundation by diving deeper into one of the most crucial aspects of leadership: strategic decision-making. In this volume, we aim to tackle the challenges leaders face in increasingly complex environments, providing you with the tools and insights necessary to make decisions that are not only effective but also impactful.

Throughout this book, you will find a blend of theory and practice—ideas supported by real-world examples and strategies that you can apply directly to your leadership scenarios. We will explore the nuances of cognitive biases, the balance of intuition and analytics, and the imperative of ethical decision-making. Each chapter is crafted to enhance your understanding and refine your decision-making skills, empowering you to lead with vision and strength.

Your insights and experiences are invaluable as we embark on this new chapter together. I invite you to engage with the material, reflect on your decision-making processes, and continue to grow as a strategic leader. Your journey to mastery in leadership is ongoing, and each step you take builds upon the last to achieve excellence.

Thank you once again for being part of this evolving narrative. Together, let's unlock the full potential of your leadership capabilities and transform every new challenge into a stepping stone to success.

TABLE OF CONTENTS

PREFACE 9

INTRODUCTION 12
    DECISION-MAKING IMPORTANCE 14
    COMMUNICATION TO DECISION-MAKING 16
    OVERVIEW OF THE BOOK'S GOALS 19

1   DECISION PSYCHOLOGY 22
    1.1   DECISION INSIGHTS 24
    1.2   BIAS AVOIDANCE 27
    1.3   INTUITION VS. ANALYSIS 30

2   SOLVING PROBLEMS 35
    2.1   PROBLEM IDENTIFICATION 37
    2.2   PROBLEM-SOLVING APPROACHES 43
    2.3   SUCCESSFUL CASE STUDIES 48

3   DATA DECISIONS 53
    3.1   DATA UTILIZATION 55
    3.2   DATA BALANCE 58
    3.3   ANALYTICAL TOOLS 60

4   RISK MANAGEMENT 66
    4.1   RISK EVALUATION 68
    4.2   RISK STRATEGIES 73
    4.3   RISK CULTURE 77

5   ETHICAL DECISIONS 82
    5.1   ETHICS UNDERSTANDING 84
    5.2   ETHICAL FRAMEWORKS 86
    5.3   ETHICAL DILEMMAS 89

6   TEAM DECISIONS 93
    6.1   GROUP FACILITATION 95
    6.2   TEAM CHALLENGES 98
    6.3   DIVERSITY LEVERAGE 101

7 DECISION SPEED 105

- 7.1 SPEED BALANCE 107
- 7.2 QUICK DECISIONS 110
- 7.3 AVOIDING PARALYSIS 113

8 COMMUNICATING DECISIONS 117

- 8.1 DECISION COMMUNICATION 119
- 8.2 HANDLING RESISTANCE 123
- 8.3 TRANSPARENCY ROLE 126

9 REFLECTING DECISIONS 130

- 9.1 IMPORTANCE OF REFLECTION 133
- 9.2 ANALYZING OUTCOMES 136
- 9.3 CONTINUOUS IMPROVEMENT: 139

10 DECISION SKILLS 143

- 10.1 PERSONAL ACTION PLAN 146
- 10.2 SKILLS DEVELOPMENT 148
- 10.3 LEADERSHIP EXAMPLE 151

11 CONCLUSION 155

- 11.1 KEY INSIGHTS 155
- 11.2 DECISION-MAKER JOURNEY 158

12 APPENDICES 162

- 12.1 EXERCISES & TOOLS 162
- 12.2 RECOMMENDED RESOURCES: 165
- 12.3 NOTES & REFERENCES 168

GRATITUDE AND NEXT STEPS 170

ACKNOWLEDGMENTS 172

ABOUT THE AUTHOR 174

WE VALUE YOUR FEEDBACK 176

EXPLORE MORE TITLES BY AUTHOR 178

PREFACE

As we navigate the complexities of the 21st century, the ability to make well-informed, strategic decisions has never been more crucial. The rapidly changing landscapes of technology, global economics, and societal expectations demand leaders who are quick to adapt and profoundly strategic in their thinking and actions. This book, "Decision Dynamics," addresses these challenges, equipping leaders like you with the necessary tools to make decisions that drive positive change and substantial impact.

In the preceding volumes of the "Leadership Transformed" series—beginning with "Leadership Awakening" and continuing through "Visionary Pathways" and "Masterful Communication"—we explored the foundational aspects of leadership from self-awareness to communication. With "Decision Dynamics," we delve into the art and science of decision-making, an essential skill that threads through every aspect of leadership.

This volume distills complex theories into practical strategies, exploring the psychological foundations and systematic approaches to decision-making. We examine cognitive influences, from biases to empowering strategies, and the critical role of data and analytics, merging quantitative analysis with qualitative judgments.

"Decision Dynamics" also addresses the human elements of decision-making within teams and organizations. It emphasizes the importance of ethical considerations, the management of risk, and the necessity of clear communication. Each chapter is designed to build on the last, providing a comprehensive toolkit that will prepare you to face not only the expected challenges of leadership but also the unforeseen ones.

Moreover, this book is about transformation. It's about transforming your approach to problems, transforming your decision-making processes, and, ultimately, transforming your leadership. It is written for current and aspiring leaders eager to master the complex yet rewarding art of strategic decision-making.

I invite you to use this book to guide your leadership journey. Apply and test the concepts in your daily professional life. Each page is designed to provoke thought, foster discussion, and challenge you to make visionary and impactful decisions.

As we progress through these pages together, I hope you will find the insights and tools provided informative and transformative, empowering you to lead with greater confidence and strategic insight.

INTRODUCTION

"In the midst of chaos, there is also opportunity." —Sun Tzu.

This timeless wisdom from Sun Tzu, the ancient Chinese military strategist, captures the essence of crisis management and decision-making that transcends centuries and continents. In moments of chaos, while many see obstacles, great leaders perceive potential. The boldest and most impactful decisions are often made within these critical junctures, reshaping the path forward and setting the foundation for significant advancements and rejuvenation.

The remarkable turnaround story of Apple Inc. under Steve Jobs is a contemporary exemplification of Sun Tzu's insight. When Jobs retook the helm of Apple in 1997, the company was teetering on the edge of bankruptcy. It faced intense competition and internal disarray, which would have doomed less resilient leaders and their companies. Jobs' return began one of the most dramatic turnarounds in business history.

Through a series of bold, decisive actions, Jobs revitalized Apple's fortunes. His first move was to streamline the product lines. Recognizing that Apple was spreading itself too thin over a confusing array of products, Jobs reduced the number of products from dozens to just a handful. This decision allowed Apple to focus on creating truly innovative and high-quality products, a principle that would become a cornerstone of the Apple brand.

Following this, Jobs spearheaded the launch of groundbreaking products that would define the tech industry for decades. The introduction of the iPod, an elegant and user-friendly device that transformed the way people consumed music, was a gamble that paid off spectacularly. It revitalized Apple and set the stage for future successes like the iPhone and iPad.

Moreover, Jobs' decision to open Apple retail stores was a direct challenge to the prevailing wisdom of the time, which favored online sales. These stores provided a controlled environment where Apple's products could be expertly showcased, and customers could experience the brand's value firsthand, enhancing customer loyalty and strength.

Each of these decisions was made amidst significant uncertainty and risk. Yet, Jobs' ability to make courageous, unconventional decisions during times of crisis underscores the profound impact that adept decision-making can have on an organization's fate. His strategic vision for Apple was not merely about surviving the storm but positioning the company at the forefront of the technology industry.

This narrative highlights the critical role of strategic decision-making in navigating corporate crises. It illustrates the broader principle that in chaos, a wealth of opportunities is ready to be seized by those leaders bold enough to take decisive action.

DECISION-MAKING IMPORTANCE

The fabric of leadership is woven with decisions that define and sometimes redefine the leader's path and, by extension, the trajectory of entire organizations and nations. History offers rich lessons on how pivotal decisions have led to monumental successes or dramatic failures.

One of the most illustrative examples is Winston Churchill during World War II. Faced with the relentless advance of Nazi forces across Europe, Churchill's decision to reject negotiation and instead commit to victory at all costs was a defining moment not only for Britain but for the modern world. His resolve rallied the British people and helped forge a determined alliance, eventually leading to the war's successful conclusion. Churchill's leadership exemplified how critical decisions under extreme pressure can have far-reaching implications.

Moving back several centuries, Queen Elizabeth I's decisions also demonstrate the impact of strategic leadership. Her choices to support naval expeditions and resist the Spanish Armada shifted England towards unprecedented expansion and influence, showcasing how decisions can extend beyond immediate military outcomes to shape a nation's economic and cultural landscapes.

In contemporary settings, decision-making is equally pivotal and often more complex due to the rapid pace of technological change and global interconnectedness. A recent example can be seen in the technology sector, where leaders like Satya Nadella of Microsoft have transformed their companies and reshaped industries through strategic decision-making. Nadella's decision to shift Microsoft's focus towards cloud computing and inclusivity within technology has not only increased Microsoft's market value but also positioned it as a leader in sustainable business practices.

Another contemporary leader, Jacinda Ardern, the Prime Minister of New Zealand, demonstrated exemplary decision-making with her immediate and effective response to the COVID-19 pandemic. Her decisions to implement strict lockdown measures and transparent communication practices saved thousands of lives, showing how timely and decisive leadership can address immediate public health crises and bolster national resilience.

These historical and contemporary examples reveal that decision-making is a multifaceted endeavor. Leaders must assess the immediate benefits and risks and consider the long-term implications of their choices on their organizations, stakeholders, and broader society. The ability to anticipate outcomes, recognize opportunities, and mitigate risks is crucial in shaping the strategies that guide these decisions.

In conclusion, the importance of decision-making in leadership cannot be overstated. It demands a blend of courage, foresight, and responsibility. As we delve deeper into "Decision Dynamics," we will explore the frameworks and tools leaders can employ to refine their decision-making processes, ensuring they can effectively navigate modern leadership's complexities.

COMMUNICATION TO DECISION-MAKING

Effective leadership transcends the ability to make good decisions; it also requires the capability to communicate those decisions effectively. The transition from mastering communication to excelling at decision-making is seamless yet profoundly significant, embodying the essence of influential leadership.

The Interdependence of Communication and Decision-Making: Decision-making involves choosing a course of action from multiple alternatives based on information and anticipated outcomes. However, the impact of those decisions dramatically depends on how they are communicated. Leaders must articulate the 'why,' 'what,' and 'how' of their decisions to garner support and guide implementation.

For instance, Martin Luther King Jr.'s effectiveness as a leader was not just due to the soundness of his decisions during the Civil Rights Movement but also his unparalleled skill in communicating these decisions. His decision to lead the March on Washington was significant. Still, his powerful delivery of the "I Have a Dream" speech mobilized supporters and brought crucial attention to the movement. This example underscores how decision-making and communication are not just sequential skills but are profoundly interwoven—effective communication amplifies the impact of a decision, driving engagement and action.

Enhancing Decision-Making Through Effective Communication: Leaders who excel in communication can clarify complex decisions, making them understandable and acceptable to a broad audience. This clarity is essential in ensuring the smooth implementation of decisions and fostering an environment where feedback and dialogue can influence ongoing and future decision-making processes.

A contemporary example is Sheryl Sandberg, whose leadership at Facebook involved crucial decisions about operational adjustments and policy changes to improve privacy and data security. Her ability to communicate these changes internally and to the public was pivotal in managing stakeholder expectations and rebuilding trust—an essential aspect following intense scrutiny over privacy concerns.

The Synergy of Skills: Furthermore, the skills involved in effective communication—listening, empathy, clarity—are also valuable in the decision-making process itself. A leader's listening ability can unveil critical insights from team discussions, customer feedback, or market trends, which are crucial for making informed decisions. Similarly, empathy allows a leader to consider decisions from the perspectives of various stakeholders, ensuring that the outcomes are beneficial on multiple fronts.

So, the transition from mastering communication to excelling at decision-making represents a critical evolution in a leader's career. This progression involves not merely acquiring a new set of skills but rather enhancing and leveraging existing communication skills to make more informed, impactful decisions. As leaders grow, recognizing and cultivating the symbiotic relationship between these skills becomes essential for fostering a culture of transparency, engagement, and collective achievement.

OVERVIEW OF THE BOOK'S GOALS

"Decision Dynamics" is meticulously designed to be more than just a manual; it is a transformative journey that equips you with the necessary skills to navigate the complexities and nuances of modern leadership. This book aims to reshape your approach to decision-making, turning it into a strategic asset that propels personal and organizational success.

Transforming Decision-Making Processes: This book's heart is the commitment to transforming how you perceive and implement decision-making processes. Traditional decision-making often follows a reactive pattern—leaders respond to challenges as they arise. "Decision Dynamics," however, encourages a more proactive approach. It equips you not only to tackle present challenges but also to anticipate future hurdles and opportunities. This shift from a reactive to a strategic stance is fundamental in today's fast-paced, ever-changing business environments.

Gaining Insights into Ethical and Impactful Decisions: Ethics play a critical role in modern decision-making. With increasing scrutiny of corporate practices and a growing demand for transparency, leaders must make decisions that adhere to legal standards and ethical norms. This book delves into frameworks and real-world scenarios that highlight how to balance complex ethical considerations, ensuring your decisions uphold integrity and foster trust among stakeholders.

Furthermore, your leadership decisions have ripple effects—impacting teams, organizations, and the broader community. "Decision Dynamics" provides the tools to ensure these decisions are impactful, fostering positive change and innovation. Through case studies, analysis, and practical applications, you will learn to implement decisions that drive success and contribute positively to your organizational culture and the wider community.

Learning to Respond with Agility and Anticipate the Future: Adaptability and agility are hallmarks of effective leadership. This book focuses on equipping you with the skills to respond swiftly and effectively to unexpected challenges. Simultaneously, it emphasizes the importance of foresight in leadership. You will learn how to foresee potential issues and opportunities through strategic planning and predictive analytics, allowing for better preparedness and more nuanced strategic planning.

Enhancing Leadership Effectiveness and Organizational Impact: Ultimately, "Decision Dynamics" aims to enhance leadership effectiveness. By refining your decision-making skills, you improve your leadership capabilities and amplify your impact on the organization. Effective decision-making leads to better resource management, improved team dynamics, increased innovation, and robust organizational performance.

As we begin our exploration through 'Decision Dynamics,' our goal is to deepen your understanding and enhance your practice of strategic decision-making. This book integrates historical insights, contemporary examples, and innovative strategies to transform how you approach challenges and opportunities. Each chapter is crafted to educate, inspire, and empower you to make ethical and effective decisions, thereby improving your leadership and organizational impact. Armed with these insights and tools, you'll be ready to lead with vision, navigate complexities confidently, and make thoughtful, impactful decisions. Let's move forward, ready to meet the evolving demands of leadership and shape the future.

1   Decision Psychology

"All men are liable to error, and most men are, in many points, by passion or interest, under temptation to it." — John Locke.

John Locke's observation highlights a timeless truth: human decision-making is inherently flawed and frequently influenced by subjective biases and emotions. This vulnerability to error becomes particularly significant in leadership, where the consequences of decisions can ripple through entire organizations or communities.

Did you know the average person makes about 35,000 remotely conscious decisions daily? This staggering number underscores the constant barrage of choices that confront us from the moment we wake up: from deciding what to wear and what to eat for breakfast to more complex decisions at work involving strategy, personnel, or finances. For leaders, the number and weight of these decisions are often magnified—each choice impacts their own lives and the lives of their employees, customers, and broader stakeholders.

Decisions are rarely simple or low-stakes for those in leadership roles. Leaders are routinely called upon to make choices under conditions of uncertainty, with incomplete information, and often under time pressure.

These decisions can determine the future direction of an organization, influence workplace culture, and impact financial stability. The complexity and ramifications of these decisions elevate the process from routine to critically strategic.

Whether minor or monumental, each decision is influenced by a complex interplay of psychology and environment. Psychological factors include cognitive biases, past experiences, emotional states, and personal values. Environmental factors encompass the external conditions and social dynamics that influence decision-making, such as organizational culture, market conditions, social norms, and technological changes.

Leaders must navigate these internal and external landscapes to make effective decisions. This requires an awareness of the typical pitfalls in decision-making and an understanding of the tools and strategies to mitigate these risks.

This chapter delves into the cognitive mechanics behind our choices, exploring how leaders can refine their decision-making prowess. We will investigate how the brain processes information and prioritizes specific data over others and how this can lead to systematic errors in thinking. By understanding these cognitive processes, leaders can develop strategies to counteract biases and improve their decision-making accuracy.

Leaders can adopt various psychological tools and frameworks to enhance their decision-making capabilities in this pursuit. Critical thinking, scenario planning, and probabilistic forecasting are invaluable for refining decision-making skills. Additionally, fostering an environment that encourages diversity of thought and constructive challenge can help leaders challenge their assumptions and make more informed choices.

1.1 DECISION INSIGHTS

Understanding how we make decisions is crucial for any leader. The human brain, a complex decision-making engine, operates through various cognitive processes influencing our everyday choices. This section explores several foundational theories and current research illuminating these processes, helping leaders make more informed and effective decisions.

Dual-Process Theories: Dual-process theory is one of the most influential frameworks in understanding decision-making. This theory, popularized by psychologist Daniel Kahneman, posits that the human mind operates using two systems. System 1 is fast, intuitive, and emotional; it makes judgments and decisions quickly and automatically, with little effort or voluntary control. System 2, however, is slower, more deliberate, and more logical. It requires conscious mental effort and is used when making complex decisions that necessitate more than a gut reaction.

For instance, a leader might use System 1 when responding to an employee's question based on a gut feeling or experience. Conversely, deciding on a new strategic direction for the company after analyzing market trends and internal data would engage System 2, as it involves deliberate analysis and critical thinking.

Heuristics and Biases: Another significant aspect of decision-making is the role of heuristics. Heuristics are mental shortcuts that help us speed up our decision-making processes. While they are often helpful, they can lead to biases—a systematic deviation from rational judgment. Common cognitive biases include:

- **Confirmation Bias:** The tendency to search for, interpret, favor, and recall information in a way that confirms one's preexisting beliefs or hypotheses.
- **Anchoring Bias:** The common human tendency to rely too heavily on the first piece of information offered (the "anchor") when making decisions.

- **Availability Heuristic:** Making a decision based on the immediate examples that come to a person's mind.

Understanding these biases and how they can skew decision-making is crucial for leaders who must make balanced and fair decisions.

Current Neuroscientific Findings: Recent advances in neuroscience have provided more profound insights into the brain's role in decision-making. Imaging techniques such as fMRI have shown how different brain regions become active during decision-making tasks. For example, the prefrontal cortex is heavily involved in planning complex cognitive behavior and expressing personality, indicating its role in System 2 processing.

Furthermore, it's empowering to know that studies have revealed how neurotransmitters like dopamine influence decision-making, impacting risk-taking and reward-based decisions. This understanding of neurobiological foundations can equip leaders to recognize their decision-making patterns and adapt strategies accordingly, fostering a sense of control and capability.

By delving into these key psychological models and neuroscientific findings, leaders can construct a practical toolkit for better decision-making. This toolkit includes techniques for mitigating biases, such as actively seeking out information that contradicts their assumptions and broadening their decision-making framework to include diverse perspectives. This practical approach can help leaders feel equipped and prepared to make better decisions.

1.2 BIAS AVOIDANCE

Biases are a universal aspect of human cognition; they serve as the brain's mechanism for simplifying information processing. While biases can sometimes be beneficial, acting as mental shortcuts that enable us to make rapid decisions, they often distort our perception. They can result in subpar decision-making if not managed. This section delves into some prevalent cognitive biases and provides practical strategies for leaders to identify and mitigate their impact.

Understanding Common Cognitive Biases

- **Confirmation Bias:** This bias manifests when individuals favor information that validates their existing beliefs or hypotheses, dismissing or underestimating evidence that contradicts them. For example, a leader might excessively highlight customer feedback that praises a new product while disregarding significant data indicating its shortcomings. This can result in persistent investment in a failing project due to a distorted perception of its success.

- **Loss Aversion:** According to Daniel Kahneman and Amos Tversky's Prospect Theory, loss aversion refers to people's tendency to prefer avoiding losses to acquiring equivalent gains. For example, leaders might avoid implementing a necessary organizational change because they overestimate its risks (losses) rather than focusing on the potential benefits (gains).
- **Anchoring Bias:** This occurs when individuals rely too heavily on the first piece of information they receive (the "anchor") when making decisions. In leadership, this might manifest when a financial forecast is unduly influenced by initial budget figures presented at the start of a negotiation, potentially leading to suboptimal financial decisions.

Practical Tips and Exercises for Bias Avoidance: To counteract these biases and enhance the objectivity of decision-making, leaders can adopt several practical measures:

- **Consider the Opposite:** Seek information that challenges your initial assumptions. For example, if you believe a project is destined to succeed, deliberately explore scenarios where it might fail.

This exercise can provide a balanced view and prepare you for potential challenges.

- **Pre-mortem Analysis:** Before finalizing a decision, conduct a pre-mortem analysis. Imagine that the decision failed and work backward to determine what might have caused it. This technique helps identify potential problems that a too-optimistic perspective could overlook.

- **Diverse Teams:** Encourage diversity in your teams, not just in demographics but also in thinking styles. Diverse teams are less likely to fall prey to groupthink and are better at identifying and challenging implicit biases.

- **Training and Awareness:** Regular training sessions on cognitive biases can help raise your team's awareness. This understanding can lead to more vigilant decision-making processes, where biases are more likely to be questioned.

- **Blind Decision-Making:** Whenever possible, use blind decision-making processes to make choices without being influenced by irrelevant information. For instance, closing your eyes to the identities of job candidates can reduce unconscious bias and help focus on the merits of their qualifications alone.

By understanding and addressing these biases, leaders can significantly enhance the accuracy and effectiveness of their decision-making. It informs leaders about what biases exist and equips them with concrete tools and strategies to overcome them, fostering a more objective, thoughtful decision-making culture within their organizations.

1.3 Intuition vs. Analysis

The balance between intuitive and analytical decision-making often defines a leader's style and effectiveness. This duality in decision-making can be seen as two ends of a spectrum, with leaders typically leaning more towards one style than the other, depending on the context, their personal experiences, and the specific demands of the situation.

Understanding Intuitive and Analytical Decision-Making

- **Intuitive Decision-Making:** Intuition is understanding something instinctively without needing conscious reasoning. It's a subconscious process informed by accumulated experiences, pattern recognition, and emotional inputs. Intuitive decisions are usually fast and often made in response to complex or incomplete information requiring swift judgment. Howard Schultz, the former CEO of Starbucks, provides a classic example of intuitive decision-making. When Schultz first walked into a Starbucks store, he immediately saw the potential for transforming it into a coffee experience rather than just a retailer of coffee beans. His intuition was not based on detailed market analysis but on his observations and the emotional impact of the coffee culture in Italy, which he felt could be replicated in the United States.

- **Analytical Decision-Making:** In contrast, analytical decision-making is characterized by a methodical evaluation of available information involving systematic analysis, data gathering, and carefully weighing potential outcomes. This style is slower but is based on rationality and often relies on quantitative data to guide decisions. Tim Cook, CEO of Apple, exemplifies analytical decision-making. Known for his meticulous attention to operational details, Cook's approach involves rigorous data analysis to ensure operational efficiency and market competitiveness. His leadership has continued Apple's legacy by emphasizing innovation based on careful, strategic planning and detailed analysis of market trends and manufacturing capabilities.

Balancing Intuition and Analysis: Effective leadership often requires a blend of intuitive and analytical approaches. Here are some strategies to optimize this balance:

- **Contextual Awareness:** Understand when to use intuition and when to rely on analysis. Quick, decisive action might favor intuition, especially in crises or when opportunities quickly arise. In contrast, decisions that shape long-term strategy or require substantial investment benefit from a more analytical approach.
- **Developing Intuitive Acuity:** Enhance your intuition by broadening your experiences, engaging with diverse perspectives, and learning from past decisions. The richer your experiences, the more accurate your intuition becomes.
- **Strengthening Analytical Skills:** Build your capacity for analytical thinking by adopting robust data analysis tools, engaging with experts, and staying informed about technological advancements that can aid in data processing and decision support.
- **Scenario Planning:** Use scenario planning to test your intuitive and analytical decisions. Imagining various outcomes based on different choices can provide insights into the potential

impacts of your decisions, blending intuition with analysis.

- **Feedback Loops:** Create mechanisms to receive feedback on the outcomes of both intuitive and analytical decisions. Feedback helps calibrate both decision-making processes, improving accuracy over time.

Dissecting and illustrating the use of intuition and analysis in leadership through the examples of Howard Schultz and Tim Cook helps leaders understand how to better harness these approaches for effective decision-making. Leaders are encouraged to cultivate a dual capacity, maximizing their strategic impact by knowing when to trust their gut and when to rely on rigorous data analysis.

As we conclude this exploration of decision psychology, it becomes evident that the art of decision-making in leadership involves a sophisticated interplay between intuition and analysis. While intuition allows leaders to make swift, experience-informed decisions in the face of ambiguity, analytical approaches provide a structured and data-driven basis for those decisions that carry long-term consequences and require thorough scrutiny. The exemplars of Howard Schultz and Tim Cook demonstrate the effectiveness of leaning into one's instinctual understanding of the market or rigorously analyzing data, respectively, each within their appropriate contexts.

For leaders aspiring to enhance their decision-making process, the journey involves cultivating a deep awareness of their natural inclinations while continuously developing the complementary skills that balance these tendencies. Leaders can build a more dynamic and resilient decision-making framework by fostering an environment where intuitive and analytical thinking are valued and developed. This framework supports the immediate needs of their roles and prepares them to face future challenges with a more nuanced and practical strategic approach. In the following chapters, we will continue building on these foundations, exploring practical strategies and tools to refine your decision-making skills further and strengthen your leadership effectiveness.

2 SOLVING PROBLEMS

"A problem well stated is a problem half-solved." — Charles Kettering.

This profound statement by Charles Kettering serves as a guiding principle for practical problem-solving, especially in leadership. It emphasizes the importance of clearly understanding and articulating a problem before attempting to solve it. This approach is vividly illustrated through the visionary actions of Elon Musk with SpaceX.

In the early 2000s, Elon Musk faced a significant challenge blocking his aspirations for space exploration: the exorbitant cost of purchasing rockets. Traditional aerospace industry explanations did not satisfy Musk's inquiry into why rockets were so expensive, with prevailing responses often rooted more in tradition than in rationale. Musk's relentless questioning and refusal to accept status quo answers led him to contemplate a radical solution—building rockets in-house.

Musk's decision to manufacture his rockets was not merely about solving a cost issue but was fundamentally about challenging and changing the established norms of the aerospace industry. By questioning the underlying causes of the high costs, Musk identified inefficiencies and outdated practices that had been unquestioned for decades. This deep understanding of the problem helped him innovate solutions that were not apparent to others.

His venture, SpaceX, aimed to reduce space travel costs by employing innovative manufacturing techniques and leveraging modern engineering technologies. The culmination of this effort was the successful launch of Falcon 1 in 2008, the first privately developed liquid-fueled rocket to reach orbit. This milestone was significant because it demonstrated the viability of reduced-cost space travel and signaled a shift in how aerospace industries could operate—more efficiently and innovatively.

Musk's leadership and problem-solving approach at SpaceX have had a profound impact. SpaceX has opened new possibilities for space exploration and commercialization by drastically reducing the cost of launching rockets. This includes reinvigorating satellite deployment, resupplying the International Space Station, and even ambitious plans for Mars colonization. Musk's work has advanced technological boundaries and inspired a new generation of companies and innovations in the aerospace sector.

Elon Musk's story is a testament to the transformative power of leadership that embraces innovative problem-solving. His approach—beginning with a clear identification and understanding of the core problem, followed by challenging conventional wisdom and culminating in groundbreaking solutions—exemplifies how leaders can effect substantial changes in their industries. Musk's journey underscores that when leaders are willing to think creatively and act boldly, even seemingly impossible challenges can be tackled effectively.

Elon Musk's journey with SpaceX exemplifies the profound impact of clear problem identification and innovative problem-solving on an industry and beyond. His approach reveals a fundamental truth in leadership: to solve a problem effectively, one must first understand it thoroughly and challenge the conventional methods that may contribute to it. As we move forward in this chapter, we will explore various problem-solving models that can help leaders identify and articulate problems with the same clarity. We will delve into different methodologies, from the analytical to the creative, and demonstrate through case studies how these strategies can be applied effectively in various scenarios. By learning to combine these approaches, leaders can enhance their ability to solve complex challenges, driving innovation and success within their organizations.

2.1 PROBLEM IDENTIFICATION

Effective leadership hinges on the ability to identify and clearly define problems. This critical first step in problem-solving often determines the success of the subsequent actions. By employing structured problem-solving models, leaders can deconstruct complex challenges into manageable components, ensuring a thorough understanding before moving toward solutions. Two powerful models often used in this phase are the "5 Whys" technique and the "Fishbone Diagram."

The 5 Whys Technique: Originally developed by Sakichi Toyoda and used extensively within Toyota Motor Corporation during the evolution of its manufacturing methodologies, the "5 Whys" technique is straightforward yet powerful. It involves asking "Why?" five times or more until the root cause of a problem is uncovered. This method is particularly effective because it helps peel away the layers of symptoms to reveal what is causing the issue. Example of the 5 Whys

Imagine a scenario where a company's delivery times are consistently delayed. The conversation might go as follows:

- Why are deliveries late? The products are not ready for shipment on time.

- Why are the products not ready on time? Production is running behind schedule.
- Why is production behind schedule? Some critical machines are frequently breaking down.
- Why are the machines breaking down? They are not being maintained according to the recommended schedule.
- Why is maintenance not performed regularly? The maintenance schedule is inconsistent with production peaks, and the current staffing levels are insufficient.

This method traces the initial symptom of late deliveries back to a root cause related to maintenance scheduling and staffing, which can be addressed directly.

Fishbone Diagram: Also known as the Ishikawa or Cause-and-Effect Diagram, the Fishbone Diagram is a visual tool for systematically exploring potential causes of a particular problem. It helps teams brainstorm and categorize problems, which is practical in complex scenarios where the contributing factors are not immediately apparent.

How to Use the Fishbone Diagram:

- **Identify the Problem:** Place the problem statement at the head (the "fish's head") and draw a horizontal line across the page (the "spine").

- **Determine the Major Categories of Causes:** Branch from the main line to create categories. Common categories include Methods, Machinery, People, Materials, Measurements, and Environment.
- **Brainstorm Causes:** For each category, identify potential causes of the problem, which branch off as smaller "bones." Teams continue asking, "Why does this happen?" within each category, adding more bones as needed.
- **Analyze the Diagram:** Once all possible causes are identified, teams can investigate further to confirm the actual root causes and prioritize solutions.

These models are invaluable in various scenarios, depending on the complexity and nature of the problem. They force a disciplined approach to problem-solving and ensure that solutions are not merely superficial but address the underlying causes. Leaders can choose a model based on the situation's specific needs, whether they require quick iterative questioning or a more detailed analysis involving multiple team members.

Leaders can choose additional problem-identification techniques depending on their specific needs and the nature of their problems. This variety ensures a comprehensive approach to problem-solving across different types of organizations and industries.

- **SWOT Analysis:** A SWOT Analysis is a strategic planning tool for identifying **Strengths, Weaknesses, Opportunities,** and **Threats** related to a business or project. This framework helps leaders understand internal and external factors impacting their objectives. By evaluating these four elements, leaders can identify areas of problems. For instance, weaknesses might highlight operational inefficiencies, while threats could pinpoint potential challenges in the market.
- **Pareto Analysis (80/20 Rule):** Pareto Analysis is based on the principle that 80% of problems are often due to 20% of causes. This technique helps identify the most significant factors contributing to a problem, allowing teams to focus their resources effectively. Useful in quality control scenarios, this method can help pinpoint the few critical issues causing most defects or problems, thereby optimizing problem-solving efforts.
- **Root Cause Analysis (RCA):** RCA is a systematic process for identifying the underlying reasons for a problem. This approach addresses the root causes rather than the symptoms,

ensuring problems are resolved. RCA can be conducted using various tools, including the previously mentioned Fishbone Diagram, but also through methodologies like Fault Tree Analysis (FTA), which uses a tree-like model to deduce failure root causes through logical analysis.

- **Brainstorming:** Brainstorming is a group creativity technique designed to generate a broad set of ideas for defining problems and their possible solutions. It encourages open and free-flowing discussion, often leading to innovative problem identification. Effective in the early stages of problem-solving, brainstorming can help uncover less obvious issues by leveraging diverse perspectives within a team.

- **Affinity Diagram:** An Affinity Diagram organizes many ideas into logical groups for review and analysis. This method is used after brainstorming to categorize and understand themes and relationships within the generated ideas. This technique can help leaders systematically group related issues and identify broader problem areas that must be addressed in complex scenarios.

- **SCAMPER:** SCAMPER is a creative problem-solving technique that provides a structured way to think through potential product or process changes. The acronym stands for Substitute, Combine, Adapt, Modify, Put to another use, Eliminate, and Reverse. By asking questions based on these verbs, leaders can uncover potential improvements or identify faulty aspects of current processes that may be causing issues.

2.2 Problem-Solving Approaches

Effective problem-solving in leadership often requires a blend of creative and analytical approaches. The choice of method depends on the nature of the problem, the desired outcome, and the context in which the problem occurs. Here, we explore the merits of each approach and provide case studies to illustrate these methods in action.

- **Analytical Approaches:** Analytical problem-solving involves a logical, systematic approach to breaking down a problem, assessing data, and applying structured techniques to arrive at a solution. It is particularly effective for well-defined problems where data is available, and the paths to resolution require precise, logical analysis. NASA often employs an analytical approach to troubleshoot issues on space missions, where precision is critical. For example, during the Apollo 13 moon mission, NASA's ground team used fault tree analysis to identify a potential explosion source in an oxygen tank. Their methodical approach guided the crew to modify the spacecraft's systems and return to Earth safely. This incident highlights how analytical problem-solving can manage complex, high-risk problems by focusing on data and structured analysis.

- **Creative Approaches:** In contrast, creative problem-solving employs more intuitive, imaginative methods that can lead to innovative solutions. Techniques like brainstorming, lateral thinking, or design thinking encourage looking at a problem from new angles and imagining what could be rather than what it currently is. A prime example of creative problem-solving is Apple's development of the iPhone. Apple's design thinking approach, which focuses on user experience and aesthetic design, led to a product that dramatically altered consumer expectations for mobile devices. By prioritizing intuitive interface design and integrating multiple functions into a single device, Apple solved the problem of cumbersome and inefficient mobile devices and redefined the smartphone market.
- **Six Sigma Approach:** Six Sigma is a data-driven problem-solving approach focusing on

process improvement and variation reduction through statistical methods. Initially developed by Motorola and popularized by General Electric, it aims to identify and eliminate manufacturing or business process defects. Under the leadership of Jack Welch, General Electric rigorously implemented Six Sigma throughout its operations. The approach improved quality across its product lines and saved billions of dollars by increasing efficiency. GE's commitment to Six Sigma became a core part of its operational strategy, significantly enhancing customer satisfaction and operational excellence.

- **TRIZ Approach:** TRIZ is a problem-solving, analysis, and forecasting tool derived from studying patterns of invention in the global patent literature. It offers a systematic approach to understanding and solving innovation problems and developing new technologies. It encourages thinking outside traditional paradigms to overcome contradictions and arrive at breakthrough solutions. Samsung has utilized TRIZ extensively to fuel its innovation process. For example, they applied TRIZ methodologies to improve the design of their washing machines. By addressing the contradiction of maintaining washing performance while reducing vibration and noise, Samsung developed a new drum technology that improved user satisfaction and product performance.

- **Design Thinking Approach**: Design thinking is a human-centered approach to innovation that integrates people's needs, technology's possibilities, and business success requirements. It encourages organizations to focus on the people they're creating for, leading to better products, services, and internal processes. Airbnb's turnaround story is a classic example of the application of design thinking. Early on, when the company was struggling to gain traction, the founders applied design thinking principles to redesign their website and improve the interface based on user experience feedback. They focused on high-quality photographs of the listings and a more intuitive booking process, which dramatically increased bookings and helped set the company on a path to success.

- **Agile Problem-Solving Approach:** Agile problem-solving adapts principles from the agile development methodology to tackle problems iteratively and incrementally. It emphasizes adaptive planning, evolutionary development, early delivery, and continual improvement, and it encourages rapid and flexible responses to change. Spotify has adopted agile methodologies in software development and problem-solving within organizational and business processes. By organizing their teams into autonomous "squads" that focus on specific aspects of the product, Spotify can quickly adapt and solve problems as they arise, fostering a responsive and dynamic business model.

The most effective leaders know when to apply a specific approach and when to combine both. For instance, they might start with a creative session to generate new ideas and then use analytical methods to test and refine them. This combination can be potent, as creative methods can generate innovative solutions, and analytical methods can implement these solutions effectively.

These approaches showcase the diversity in problem-solving methods and underline the importance of choosing the right strategy based on the specific problem, organizational culture, and desired outcomes. Each case study illustrates how effectively applied problem-solving strategies can lead to substantial organizational improvements and innovations.

Practical Tips for Choosing the Right Approach

- **Define the Problem Clearly:** Understanding whether the problem is open-ended or specific can guide whether a creative or analytical approach is more appropriate.

- **Consider the Available Data:** An analytical approach might be more suitable if substantial data is available. Creative methods might yield better solutions if the problem is new or the data is scant.
- **Evaluate the Urgency:** Straightly analytical methods might be necessary to devise a solution quickly. Spending time on creative thinking could lead to more innovative and impactful solutions for long-term issues.
- **Leverage Team Strengths:** Consider your team's strengths. Teams with strong analytical skills may prefer data-driven approaches, while creative teams prefer brainstorming and lateral thinking.
- **Iterate as Needed:** Problem-solving is often an iterative process. Leaders should be prepared to cycle through different approaches as they learn more about the problem and refine their solutions.

This detailed examination of problem-solving approaches highlights the value of creative and analytical thinking in leadership. By understanding the nuances of each approach and learning from real-world applications like those at NASA and Apple, leaders can enhance their ability to tackle complex problems effectively.

2.3 SUCCESSFUL CASE STUDIES

Applying problem-solving techniques can dramatically enhance a leader's ability to address and resolve challenges effectively. This section highlights successful case studies and introduces a workshop or simulation to allow readers to apply the problem-solving skills discussed directly. Engaging in this hands-on activity will help solidify the concepts and encourage active learning and application of these methods in real-world situations.

Workshop Scenario: Reviving a Failing Product Line: Imagine being a product manager at a company with a once-popular product line experiencing declining sales and negative customer feedback. The task is to identify the root causes of the product line's failure and develop potential solutions to revive it.

Workshop Steps

1. **Identify the Problem:** Clearly define the problem with the product line. What exactly are the symptoms of the decline? Is it a decrease in sales, poor customer reviews, or something else?

2. **Apply the 5 Whys Technique:** Use the 5 Whys technique to dig deeper into the initial symptoms identified. For example:
    a. Why have sales dropped? (Product has become technologically outdated.)
    b. Why has the product become outdated? (Innovation has been slow.)
    c. Why has innovation been slow? (R&D budget cuts.)
    d. Why were there R&D budget cuts? (Shift in strategic focus towards other products.)
    e. Why was there a strategic shift? (Market trends indicated high growth in another sector.)
3. **Use the Fishbone Diagram:** Employ the Fishbone Diagram to analyze the problem further, focusing on categories like Processes, People, Tools, and External Factors. Participants should brainstorm possible causes under each category that might contribute to the product line's failure. For instance, under Processes, issues might include outdated manufacturing techniques; under People, perhaps there's a lack of skills in the current workforce; under Tools, maybe there's inadequate technology support; and under External Factors, consider new competitors or changing regulations.

4. **Develop Solutions:** Based on the insights from the 5 Whys and the Fishbone Diagram, brainstorm potential solutions for each identified root cause. For example, if slow innovation due to R&D budget cuts is a root cause, one solution could be reallocating budgets or seeking external funding.
5. **Plan Implementation:** Choose the most viable solutions and create a short implementation plan. Consider what resources will be needed, who will be responsible, and how success will be measured.
6. **Role-Playing:** Participants can role-play stakeholders involved in the decision-making process, such as the CEO, CFO, and product managers. This will help them understand different perspectives and anticipate potential objections or support.
7. **Feedback and Reflection:** After role-playing, gather feedback on the solutions from all participants. Discuss what might realistically work and refine the plan accordingly.
8. **Simulation Debrief:** Conclude the workshop with a debrief session where participants reflect on their knowledge about applying these problem-solving techniques. Encourage sharing insights on how these methods can be adapted to real-world challenges.

This workshop scenario provides an engaging way for you to apply problem-solving skills and helps them understand the practical aspects of implementing these techniques in a business context. By working through this simulation, participants can better appreciate how structured problem-solving can lead to successful outcomes in complex situations.

As we conclude our problem-solving exploration, it's evident that this art involves more than just reactive measures. Leaders can address issues and drive sustainable growth by strategically applying models like the 5 Whys and Fishbone Diagram and creative and analytical approaches. This chapter's case studies and workshops show that the right tools and methods can turn daunting challenges into opportunities. Leaders should share these insights with their teams and incorporate them into strategic thinking to refine problem-solving skills continually. Organizations can navigate an evolving business landscape by fostering a culture of detailed analysis, creativity, and continuous improvement and transforming obstacles into stepping stones for success.

3 DATA DECISIONS

"Without data, you're just another person with an opinion." —W. Edwards Deming.

In modern business, data is more than just numbers and stats; it's the foundation of strategic decision-making. Amazon, a titan in the e-commerce industry, demonstrates the profound impact of data-driven decisions. By harnessing extensive consumer data, Amazon has refined its operational strategies and revolutionized how products are marketed and delivered to consumers worldwide. Through sophisticated algorithms and analytics, Amazon personalizes customer experiences, predicts purchasing behaviors, and manages vast inventories with unprecedented precision. This capacity for personalization and efficiency has significantly elevated customer satisfaction and streamlined Amazon's operational effectiveness, setting a benchmark in the industry. The practical benefits of this approach are clear: increased customer satisfaction, improved operational efficiency, and a competitive edge in the market.

Amazon's approach symbolizes data's transformative power in today's business environment. Data-driven decision-making enables organizations to move from guesswork and assumptions to a model where verifiable data substantiate choices. This shift enhances accuracy in strategy and planning and provides a competitive edge in rapidly changing markets.

This chapter delves deep into the mechanics and strategies of data utilization, highlighting how leaders can leverage this asset to propel their organizations forward. As we explore data integration into business processes, we focus on how data can be used to make informed, objective, and impactful decisions. We examine the tools and methodologies leaders need to effectively gather, analyze, and interpret data, ensuring that their decisions are based on solid evidence rather than intuition alone. As a leader, it's up to you to champion this change and guide your organization toward a data-driven future.

Data-driven decision-making extends beyond customer interactions and inventory management. It encompasses various aspects of business operations, from financial forecasting and risk management to employee engagement and resource allocation. By effectively using data, leaders can anticipate market trends, mitigate risks, and identify opportunities for innovation and growth.

Moreover, this chapter addresses the challenges and responsibilities accompanying data use, including data privacy concerns, the ethical use of information, and the need for data literacy within organizations. As businesses increasingly rely on data, leaders must also foster a culture that values and understands the significance of data integrity and ethical handling.

3.1 Data Utilization

In the digital age, the ability to effectively harness data is a crucial differentiator for successful organizations. Leaders need robust data collection and analysis understanding to make informed decisions that drive growth and innovation. To effectively utilize data, leaders must first master the art of data collection and analysis. This involves several crucial steps:

- **Identifying Key Data Points:** Leaders must identify which data points are essential for strategic decisions. This requires a deep understanding of business operations and the questions that need answering. For example, a retail leader might focus on customer purchase histories and product inventory levels, whereas a healthcare executive might prioritize patient outcomes and treatment efficacies.
- **Choosing the Right Tools:** Various tools and software are available for data collection and analysis. Customer Relationship Management (CRM) systems are vital for tracking customer

interactions and gathering data on their behaviors and preferences, which can inform marketing strategies and customer service improvements. Enterprise Resource Planning (ERP) systems integrate various business processes—such as finance, HR, and supply chain—into a single system, providing comprehensive insights that can enhance operational efficiencies.

- **Leveraging Advanced Analytics Platforms:** Specialized analytics platforms like Tableau or Google Analytics offer potent data visualization and web analytics capabilities for deeper insights. These tools allow leaders to see patterns and trends in data that might not be obvious from raw numbers alone, enabling more nuanced interpretations and smarter strategic decisions.

Let us understand Data utilization with a Case Study of Netflix. Netflix's use of data analytics offers a compelling case study on how data can drive decision-making in creative and operational contexts. Netflix collects vast amounts of data on viewer activities, including what they watch, when they pause or stop, and how they rate content. By analyzing these data points, Netflix can uncover detailed insights into viewer preferences and viewing patterns.

- **Strategic Content Decisions:** Using data analytics, Netflix decides how to recommend content to users and what content to create. For instance, the decision to produce "House of Cards" was based on data indicating a significant overlap in the audience that enjoyed Kevin Spacey films, the original British series of the same name, and director David Fincher's work. The series' success validated Netflix's data-driven content strategy, demonstrating that leveraging data can lead to highly successful outcomes in content creation.
- **Operational Efficiency:** Netflix also uses data to optimize its streaming quality and bandwidth usage, which are critical for customer satisfaction and operational cost management. By analyzing data on streaming performance across different devices and network conditions, Netflix can fine-tune its compression algorithms to deliver the best possible viewing experience at the lowest necessary bandwidth.

By examining how Netflix uses data, leaders can see the value of strategic data collection and analysis in improving decision-making and creating innovative strategies that respond to consumer behaviors and preferences. This example lays the groundwork for combining quantitative data with qualitative insights for better decision-making.

3.2 DATA BALANCE

While data-driven decision-making has transformed how organizations operate and compete, leaders must recognize that relying solely on data can lead to pitfalls. This section explores the inherent limitations of data and the importance of integrating data-driven insights and human judgment to make balanced and effective decisions. Data, as robust as it is, comes with inherent limitations that leaders need to be aware of:

- **Data Quality Issues:** Decisions are only as accurate and reliable as the data on which they are based. Issues like incomplete data sets, erroneous entries, and outdated information can skew analysis and lead to poor decisions. Ensuring data quality involves rigorous data management practices, including regular audits and validations.
- **Bias in Data Collection:** Data isn't immune to bias, mainly if the data collection methods are flawed. For example, if a survey is designed with leading questions or the sample doesn't represent the broader population, the resulting data will carry these biases. Leaders must critically

evaluate the methods used to collect data to ensure they are fair and unbiased.

- **Potential for Misinterpretation:** Data can be complex, and interpretation is not always straightforward. Misinterpreting data trends or correlations can lead to misguided strategies. Leaders must have a solid understanding of statistical methods and be cautious of concluding without sufficient evidence or statistical significance.

To overcome the limitations of data, it is imperative for leaders to adopt a holistic approach to decision-making:

- **Integrating Quantitative Data and Qualitative Insights:** Effective decision-making involves blending complex data with soft insights. This means complementing quantitative analysis with qualitative data, such as employee opinions, customer feedback, and experiential knowledge. For instance, while customer data may show a decline in product satisfaction, direct customer interviews might reveal underlying causes like perceived value or customer service issues that are not evident from numbers alone.
- **Valuing Human Intuition and Experience:** Human intuition, borne out of experience and tacit knowledge, plays a critical role in

interpreting data and filling the gaps that data cannot address. Leaders should value insights gathered from years of experience in the field, which can provide context that raw data might miss.

- **Scenario Planning:** Employing scenario planning can help leaders envision various outcomes based on mixed quantitative data and qualitative judgment. This technique allows leaders to test the robustness of their decisions against multiple futures and to develop flexible and adaptable strategies.

- **Ethical Considerations:** Leaders must weigh the moral implications alongside the data in decisions that impact human lives or involve sensitive ethical questions. Decisions in areas like AI deployment in HR or customer data usage for marketing require a careful balance between what data says is possible and what is ethically correct.

By addressing the limits of data and emphasizing the need for a holistic decision-making approach, leaders can ensure that their decisions are informed by the best available data and guided by ethical considerations and human insight. This balanced approach is crucial for making decisions that are effective, responsible, and aligned with organizational values and societal expectations.

3.3 ANALYTICAL TOOLS

Analytical tools play a crucial role in data-driven decision-making. Regression analysis is a versatile method widely used across industries to discern relationships between variables and predict future outcomes. This section provides a comprehensive step-by-step guide to conducting regression analysis, followed by a practical application example. Here is the Step-by-Step Guide to Regression Analysis:

Data Preparation:

- **Collecting Data:** Gather the necessary data involving the dependent variable (what you want to predict) and independent variables (factors that might influence that prediction).
- **Cleaning Data:** Cleaning data by removing or correcting anomalies or errors. This may involve missing values, outliers, or incorrect data entries.
- **Transforming Data:** Depending on the requirement, you might need to transform your data (e.g., logarithmic transformation) to meet the regression analysis assumptions.

Choosing the Right Type of Regression:

- **Simple Linear Regression:** Use if there is one independent variable.
- **Multiple Linear Regression:** Use if there are multiple independent variables.
- **Logistic Regression:** Use if the dependent variable is categorical.

Running the Analysis:

- **Using Software:** Tools like SPSS, Excel, R, or Python are commonly used for regression analysis. Set up your data in these programs and use built-in functions to run the regression.
- **Configuring Models:** Input your dependent and independent variables into the model. If you suspect the effects of one variable depend on another, you can configure additional settings, such as entering interaction terms.

Interpreting the Results:

- **Coefficients:** Analyze the coefficients to understand the influence of each independent variable on the dependent variable.
- **R-squared Value:** Look at the R-squared value to understand how much of the variance in your dependent variable is explained by the independent variables.

- **P-values:** Check the p-values to determine the statistical significance of your findings.

Let us understand the Case Study of a Retail Company Using Regression Analysis. Consider a retail company that wants to predict future sales volumes. The company used multiple linear regression analysis to understand how different factors such as marketing spend, seasonality, and economic conditions impact sales.

Setting Up the Model:

- **Dependent Variable:** Monthly sales volume.
- **Independent Variables:** Monthly marketing spend, a dummy variable for seasonality (1 for high season, 0 for low season), and economic indicators such as consumer confidence index.
- **Data Collection and Preparation:** Data is collected from past sales records, marketing budgets, and publicly available economic data.

The data is cleaned to ensure accuracy, and seasonality is coded correctly.

- **Analysis:** The regression analysis is run using a software tool, and the model's coefficients indicate that while marketing spending has a positive effect on sales, the impact of seasonality is even more significant, especially during the high season. Economic conditions also play a role but to a lesser extent.

- **Interpretation and Action:** Based on the analysis, the retail company decides to increase its marketing budget during the high season to capitalize on the increased seasonal demand and adjust its inventory levels more accurately according to predicted sales volumes.

This detailed guide and practical application demonstrate how regression analysis can be a powerful tool for leaders to make informed decisions based on quantitative data. Organizations can enhance their strategic planning and resource allocation by understanding and applying these techniques, leading to more effective and efficient operations.

As we wrap up our discussion on data decisions, it's clear that strategic data use is crucial for organizational success. This chapter covered the mechanics of data utilization, the balance between data and intuition, and the use of advanced analytical tools. Leaders can convert information into actionable insights for informed decision-making by effectively gathering, analyzing, and interpreting data. However, it's vital to recognize data's limits and blend it with experiential knowledge to make compassionate and contextually relevant decisions. Leaders should cultivate a culture that values data-driven insights yet maintains a holistic view, equipping their organizations to navigate the complexities of today's business world. These principles will boost operational efficiency and strengthen strategic initiatives, keeping your organization resilient and competitive.

4 RISK MANAGEMENT

"Only those who dare to fail greatly can achieve greatly."
—Robert F. Kennedy.

This quote by Robert F. Kennedy encapsulates the essence of risk-taking in leadership. The stories of Howard Schultz with Starbucks and Coca-Cola's New Coke adventure vividly illustrate the spectrum of risk outcomes. When Howard Schultz purchased Starbucks in the late 1980s, the company was a regional coffee bean retailer with only 60 stores. Schultz saw a more significant potential, envisioning a transformation of these outlets into a completely new concept—cafes that sold excellent coffee and doubled as inviting spaces encouraging social interaction, drawing inspiration from Italian coffee culture. Despite the considerable risk of deviating from a profitable, established business model and the looming possibility of failure, Schultz proceeded. His vision and willingness to take significant risks ultimately redefined global coffee culture and expanded Starbucks into one of the world's most recognizable brands.

In stark contrast stands the case of New Coke, introduced by Coca-Cola in 1985. In an attempt to reinvigorate its brand and combat losing market share to Pepsi, Coca-Cola developed a new formula. Despite extensive taste tests that reportedly favored the new flavor, the public's reaction to replacing the original formula was overwhelmingly negative. The backlash was swift and brutal, significantly hurting the brand's image and forcing the company to revert to its original formula within months. This episode is a cautionary tale of how even well-researched risks can backfire, particularly when they misjudge public sentiment and consumer attachment to a product.

The Dual Nature of Risk

These contrasting outcomes underscore a fundamental truth about risk: it is a double-edged sword capable of yielding great rewards or inducing significant setbacks. Effective risk management requires understanding and balancing these potential outcomes. It involves the courage to take risks when opportunities arise and the wisdom to foresee and mitigate possible downsides.

Exploring Risk Management in Business

This chapter delves into the complexities of risk management within a business context. Risk management does not eliminate risk but involves making strategic decisions that optimize outcomes. Effective risk management protects organizations against potential losses and positions them to capitalize on opportunities that might otherwise be missed due to a fear of failure.

- **Risk Evaluation:** We will examine methodologies for identifying and assessing risks, using real-world examples from various industries to illustrate how different organizations approach risk evaluation.
- **Risk Strategies:** This section discusses mitigating risk, including developing and implementing a robust risk management framework that aligns with the organization's strategic objectives.
- **Risk Culture:** Finally, we address the importance of cultivating a risk-aware culture within organizations, highlighting practical steps and organizational strategies that encourage proactive risk management.

By the end of this chapter, you will gain insights into the principles of risk management that are essential for navigating the uncertainties of the business world. You will learn how to approach risk not as something to be feared and avoided but as an integral part of strategic decision-making that, when managed effectively, can lead to substantial benefits and a solid competitive advantage.

4.1 RISK EVALUATION

Effective risk management begins with identifying potential risks. This critical first step sets the stage for all subsequent risk management efforts. It is integral to developing a proactive strategy that safeguards an organization while enabling it to seize opportunities.

Identifying risks involves a comprehensive and systematic analysis to determine where, how, and why things might go wrong. Employing strategic tools can provide a structured approach to uncovering these risks:

- **SWOT Analysis:** This tool assesses an organization's internal Strengths and Weaknesses, along with external Opportunities and Threats. It helps leaders understand what advantages they can leverage, vulnerabilities they need to mitigate, where the most excellent opportunities lie, and which threats could impact operations.
- **PEST Analysis:** By examining Political, Economic, Social, and Technological factors, this analysis helps organizations identify big-picture risks that could impact business strategies. Each factor can affect an organization's operations and must be considered to ensure comprehensive risk identification.
- **Failure Mode and Effects Analysis (FMEA):** FMEA is a systematic, proactive method for evaluating a process to identify where and how it might fail and to assess the relative impact of

different failures to identify the parts of the process that most need change. It involves reviewing components, assemblies, and subsystems to identify failure modes and their causes. Widely used in manufacturing but applicable in any industry, FMEA helps anticipate potential points of failure, allowing organizations to implement strategies to mitigate these risks before they become a problem.

- **Risk Register:** A risk register is a tool to document risks, their severity, and the steps to manage their probability. It acts as a central repository for all risks identified within the project or organization, providing an ongoing overview of risks and their status. A risk register is an essential tool for tracking identified risks, associated mitigation strategies, and responsible parties and is helpful in project management and ongoing operations.

- **Monte Carlo Simulation:** This technique uses probability modeling to predict the impact of risk and uncertainty in project management, financial forecasting, and other planning activities. It allows leaders to see all the possible outcomes of their decisions and assess the impact of risk, allowing for better decision-making under uncertainty. Particularly valuable in finance and insurance, Monte Carlo simulations can also be used in project management, supply chain, and any other field requiring decision-making under uncertainty.

- **Bowtie Method:** The Bowtie method is a risk management tool that provides a visual diagram to analyze and demonstrate causal relationships in high-risk scenarios. It visually maps out the path from potential causes to prevention and mitigation measures, the risk event, and its potential consequences. Often used in the energy, mining, and aerospace sectors, it helps visualize complex risk scenarios and effectively communicates how risks are managed.
- **Heat Maps:** Risk heat maps are visual representations that use color coding to illustrate the level of risk associated with different areas and processes within the organization. They help quickly communicate insights into the risks, highlighting areas that need urgent attention. Heat maps are applicable across various industries to present a snapshot of risk distribution across different business units, helping executives prioritize and make informed decisions.

- **Delphi Technique:** The Delphi Technique estimates the likelihood and outcome of future events. A panel of experts' answers questionnaires in two or more rounds. After each round, a facilitator anonymously summarizes the experts' forecasts and reasons. The experts are encouraged to revise their earlier answers in light of the replies of other panel members. It is used for risk identification and forecasting in complex scenarios where subjective judgments must be pooled, typically in technological forecasting, policy determination, and risk management.

These techniques allow leaders to capture a broad spectrum of potential risks, encompassing both internal operational risks and external strategic risks.

Once risks are identified, the next crucial step is their evaluation. This involves analyzing each identified risk regarding its potential impact on the organization and the likelihood of its occurrence. Practical risk evaluation helps prioritize risks, focusing resources and attention where they are most needed.

A standard tool used in risk evaluation is the risk matrix, which helps categorize risks by their impact severity and probability of occurrence. This visual tool enables decision-makers to ascertain which risks pose the greatest threat quickly and thus require more immediate attention or robust planning.

A risk evaluation might focus on patient safety in the healthcare industry. The risk of infection during procedures requires stringent controls or compliance with new health regulations, which, if not adhered to, could lead to severe penalties and damage to reputation.

For financial institutions, the emphasis might be on cyber security risks, where data breaches could lead to significant financial loss and erosion of customer trust, or on compliance risks linked to global ever-changing financial regulations.

By evaluating risks using these structured approaches, organizations can respond more effectively to challenges and anticipate and prepare for potential threats, enhancing their resilience. Risk evaluation is not a one-time task but a dynamic process that requires ongoing attention as new risks emerge and existing risks evolve.

This detailed explanation of the "Risk Evaluation" process in risk management equips leaders with the necessary tools and methodologies to identify and evaluate risks comprehensively. It highlights the importance of structured, strategic approaches to manage risks effectively, ensuring that organizations survive and thrive in an uncertain environment.

4.2 RISK STRATEGIES

Once risks are thoroughly evaluated, organizations must focus on developing and implementing strategies to mitigate them effectively. This crucial phase in risk management aims to minimize the likelihood of risk occurrence and lessen potential impacts if they do manifest. The chosen strategies may vary based on the nature of the risk, industry standards, and the organization's risk tolerance.

Risk Mitigation involves selecting and applying the most appropriate tools and strategies to manage identified risks. Common strategies include:

- **Risk Avoidance** involves altering plans to sidestep the risk or withdraw from the risky activity. For instance, a company might avoid entering a market with unstable political conditions to circumvent potential losses.
- **Risk Reduction:** This strategy seeks to reduce the likelihood and impact of a risk. Examples include regular maintenance on machinery to prevent breakdowns or thorough training for employees to avoid workplace accidents.
- **Risk Transfer:** Transferring risk involves shifting the risk to another party, typically through insurance or outsourcing. A software company might use a cloud service provider to

mitigate the risk of data loss, or a construction firm might obtain insurance to cover the costs of potential structural failures.

- **Risk Acceptance:** This is chosen when the mitigation costs exceed the potential loss, or the risk is so minor that it can be managed as a regular cost of doing business. A business may accept the risk of a low-probability supply chain disruption if the cost of creating redundant suppliers is prohibitive.

Implementing a Risk Management Framework

A systematic risk management approach is essential for embedding risk mitigation into the organizational fabric. A robust risk management framework includes:

- **Policies and Procedures:** Establish clear policies that define how risks are identified, assessed, managed, and monitored. These policies should align with the organization's objectives and regulatory requirements.
- **Roles and Responsibilities:** Delineate roles and responsibilities for risk management to ensure accountability. This should include everyone from the board members to operational staff, detailing who is responsible for which actions in the risk management process.

- **Risk Assessment Processes:** Develop and implement processes for ongoing risk assessment that allow for the continuous identification and evaluation of new and evolving risks. This includes regular risk audits and reviews.
- **Response Strategies:** Outline specific strategies and action plans for responding to risks based on their severity. This should include proactive strategies to prevent risk and reactive strategies to respond to risk events.
- **Communication and Reporting:** Ensure that effective communication and reporting mechanisms allow for timely dissemination of risk information within the organization. This helps maintain transparency and aids in quick response and adaptation to risk exposure.
- **Training and Awareness:** Conduct regular training sessions to raise awareness about the importance of risk management and ensure that all employees are familiar with the processes involved in identifying and responding to risks.

By developing and implementing a comprehensive risk management framework, organizations can ensure they are prepared to handle adverse events and positioned to make informed decisions that balance risks with potential rewards. This proactive approach safeguards the organization's assets and reputation and contributes to its strategic success and resilience.

4.3 RISK CULTURE

Creating a risk-aware culture within an organization is more than a strategic imperative; it is a fundamental necessity that can determine the long-term sustainability and resilience of the enterprise. This culture enhances the ability to deal with risks proactively and embeds risk considerations into the fabric of organizational decision-making.

Building a Risk-Aware Culture: Building a risk-aware culture involves several key components:

- **Employee Training and Awareness:** Education is critical in fostering a risk-aware culture. Regular training sessions should be conducted to ensure that all employees understand the basics of risk management, recognize the common risks associated with their work, and know the procedures to follow when a risk is identified. This training should also emphasize the importance of risk management in achieving the organization's overall strategic objectives.
- **Promoting Open Communication:** A culture that encourages open communication about risks

enables issues to be addressed more quickly and effectively. Establishing a non-punitive reporting environment where employees feel safe to report risks without fear of retribution is essential. This can be facilitated through regular meetings, feedback mechanisms, and an organizational structure that supports and rewards transparency.

- **Embedding Risk in Decision-Making:** Risk considerations should be integral to all decision-making processes. Risk assessments must be a standard agenda item in strategic planning sessions, project meetings, and daily operations. Leaders should consistently ask about the risks associated with each decision and consider risk mitigation strategies in their planning.

Practical Steps and Organizational Strategies: To practically implement a risk-aware culture, organizations can undertake the following steps:

- **Regular Risk Training Sessions:** Implementing an ongoing schedule of risk training sessions can help keep risk awareness high and ensure new employees are quickly brought up to speed. These sessions can cover various topics, from identifying and assessing risks to the correct procedures for mitigating and reporting risks.

- **Clear Communication Channels:** Establishing clear and accessible channels for communicating about risks is vital. This might include dedicated risk management hotlines, specialized email addresses for reporting risks, or regular open forums where employees can discuss potential risks with management.
- **Integration of Risk Management into Strategic Planning:** Ensure that risk management is embedded into the strategic planning process at all levels. This can involve using risk assessment templates and checklists during the planning stages of any new project or strategic initiative.
- **Adoption of Enterprise Risk Management (ERM) Software:** Investing in robust ERM software can dramatically improve an organization's ability to track and manage risks. These systems provide a centralized platform for recording and analyzing risks, generating reports, and monitoring the effectiveness of risk management strategies across various departments. They enhance visibility and

response times, crucial for effective risk management.

- **Fostering Leadership Commitment:** Leadership must exemplify and champion risk management practices. When leaders consistently prioritize and talk about risk management, it sends a clear message to the entire organization about its importance.

By fostering a risk-aware culture, organizations safeguard their assets, ensure compliance with regulations, and enhance their capacity to seize opportunities that carry risk. A well-established risk culture is characterized by preparedness, informed decision-making, and an inherent resilience that can significantly contribute to the organization's success and longevity.

As we conclude our discussion on risk management, it's clear that effective risk management is crucial for proactive leadership. It enables organizations to handle uncertainties and capitalize on opportunities. This chapter has outlined vital risk evaluation techniques, strategies, and the importance of a risk-aware culture, helping leaders steer their organizations through challenges. Armed with these tools and insights, you can integrate risk management into your leadership to turn potential threats into growth opportunities and gain a competitive edge.

5   ETHICAL DECISIONS

"Ethics is knowing the difference between what you have a right to do and what is right to do." —Potter Stewart.

The Cambridge Analytica scandal that enveloped Facebook in April 2018 starkly illustrates modern businesses' intricate ethical dilemmas. The scandal involved exploiting personal data from over 87 million Facebook users without their consent to influence political outcomes. This breach highlighted critical questions about tech companies' responsibilities in protecting user data and their role in safeguarding or undermining democratic processes.

As the scandal unfolded, it became evident that Facebook's data privacy measures were insufficient, leading to a significant erosion of public trust. The backlash was swift and severe, with Facebook experiencing a substantial drop in its stock value and facing intense scrutiny from the public and legislators worldwide. This event catalyzed a broader discussion about digital privacy rights and corporations' ethical obligations in the information age.

The scandal's repercussions extended beyond Facebook's immediate financial losses. It triggered a global reevaluation of data privacy regulations, prompting governments worldwide to tighten legislation to protect individuals' information. The European Union's General Data Protection Regulation (GDPR), which came into effect shortly after the scandal, exemplifies these changes, offering users more control over their data and imposing stringent penalties for violations.

This scandal underscores the complex ethical landscape businesses navigate in the digital age. Companies, especially those dealing with vast amounts of user data, find themselves at a crossroads between leveraging that data for business gains and respecting the ethical implications of their data use practices. It highlights a crucial lesson for all leaders: ethical breaches can have far-reaching consequences on a company's reputation, legal standing, and bottom line.

As we delve deeper into this chapter, we will explore how leaders can develop and implement robust ethical frameworks within their organizations to prevent such breaches. Understanding the difference between legal compliance and ethical responsibility will be central to our discussions, guiding leaders in ensuring their decisions adhere to regulations and uphold the highest moral standards. This journey through ethical decision-making will arm leaders with the necessary tools to foster a culture of integrity and trust, which is paramount in retaining stakeholder confidence and securing long-term success.

5.1 ETHICS UNDERSTANDING

Ethical decision-making is rooted in a deep philosophical tradition that explores the fundamental nature of morally sound choices. This understanding is essential for leaders who must navigate the complex ethical dilemmas of the modern business environment. To fully grasp the role of ethics in decision-making, it is vital to understand the philosophical underpinnings that have shaped ethical thought over centuries:

- **Utilitarianism:** Developed by philosophers like Jeremy Bentham and John Stuart Mill, utilitarianism is an ethical theory that suggests that the best action is the one that maximizes utility, usually defined as that which produces the greatest well-being of the most significant number of people. This approach can guide leaders in decisions that affect their stakeholders broadly, such as environmental policies that benefit the community or pricing strategies that balance profit with customer satisfaction.
- **Deontological Ethics:** Formulated by Immanuel Kant, deontological ethics is an approach that focuses on whether an action is right or wrong under a series of rules rather than its consequences. It encourages leaders to adhere to their duties and obligations when making

decisions, such as maintaining honesty in financial reporting or committing to fair labor practices, regardless of the potential business outcomes.

- **Virtue Ethics:** In Aristotle's philosophies, virtue ethics emphasizes the virtues, or moral character, of the individual involved in the act rather than the ethics of the act itself. This perspective might lead a company to focus on cultivating leadership traits such as integrity and generosity, viewing these character qualities as crucial for long-term ethical behavior within the organization.

In addition to these traditional theories, modern ethical frameworks offer additional perspectives that are particularly relevant in today's diverse and fast-paced world:

- **Rights-Based Approaches:** These approaches prioritize the rights and freedoms of individuals, asserting that certain rights (such as the right to privacy or freedom from discrimination) should not be violated regardless of the outcome. This framework can guide policies related to consumer data protection, where individual privacy rights must be safeguarded, even if leveraging such data could benefit the business.

- **Fairness or Justice Theories:** Often associated with philosopher John Rawls, these theories focus on ensuring fairness and justice, particularly regarding equal opportunity and resource distribution. Such theories could influence decisions regarding equitable pay, diversity and inclusion initiatives, or fair access to company advancement opportunities.

The above ethical philosophies equip leaders with diverse tools for analyzing and resolving the ethical challenges they face in their roles. By understanding and applying these principles, leaders can ensure that their decisions drive business success and uphold the highest standards of moral integrity, fostering trust and loyalty among all stakeholders.

5.2 ETHICAL FRAMEWORKS

Navigating the ethical complexities of modern leadership requires more than a theoretical understanding of philosophical principles; it demands practical frameworks and guidelines that can be directly applied in day-to-day decision-making. Here, we explore these frameworks, providing leaders with tools to ensure their decisions reflect moral integrity and promote an ethical corporate culture.

Guidelines for Ethical Decision-Making

- **Four Component Model**: Developed by James Rest, the Four Component Model breaks down the ethical decision-making process into four key components: **moral sensitivity** (recognizing the moral issues), **moral judgment** (determining the correct action), **moral motivation** (prioritizing moral values over other values), and **moral character** (implementing the chosen ethical action). This model can be instrumental in complex scenarios of unclear ethical dilemmas. For instance, a leader might use moral sensitivity to recognize how a marketing campaign might mislead customers, employ moral judgment to revise the campaign's messaging, find the moral motivation to prioritize transparency and use moral character to implement the changes despite potential pushback or increased costs.
- **Ethical Decision-Making Frameworks:** Implementing a structured decision-making process can also help navigate ethical dilemmas. Typical steps include identifying the ethical issue, gathering information, evaluating the actions from various ethical perspectives, deciding, and reflecting on the outcome. Tools such as ethical decision trees or checklists can systematically guide leaders through these steps, ensuring that all relevant factors are considered.

Incorporating Ethics into Corporate Governance

- **Codes of Ethics:** Developing and enforcing a code of ethics is crucial for embedding ethical standards within an organization. This code should outline expected behaviors, provide examples of acceptable and unacceptable actions, and detail the mechanisms for addressing ethical breaches. A well-articulated code of ethics is a guideline for individual behavior and a benchmark for the entire organization's ethical climate.
- **Corporate Social Responsibility (CSR) Policies:** CSR policies that align with the company's core values and business model can effectively integrate ethical considerations into daily business operations. These policies should address critical areas such as environmental responsibility, social equity, and economic impact. By committing to CSR, companies can enhance their reputations, attract and retain top talent, and improve stakeholder relationships.
- **Compliance Mechanisms:** Effective governance requires robust compliance mechanisms that ensure adherence to legal and ethical standards. These might include regular ethics training, anonymous reporting systems,

and strong whistleblower protections. Regular audits and reviews of ethical practices help ensure these mechanisms are not merely symbolic but actively enforce the organization's ethical standards.

The above frameworks equip leaders with the tools necessary to make decisions that comply with legal standards and uphold and advance ethical practices within their organizations. They provide detailed frameworks and guidelines for ethical decision-making and embed these principles into corporate governance. These strategies foster an environment of trust and integrity, which is crucial for sustaining long-term success in today's business landscape.

5.3 Ethical Dilemmas

Navigating ethical dilemmas effectively is crucial for leadership, as these challenging situations often test a leader's values and decision-making skills under pressure. To aid in developing these critical skills, this section employs role-playing scenarios that simulate real-world ethical challenges, followed by analysis and reflection to deepen understanding and improve ethical reasoning.

Role-Playing Scenarios

- **Conflict of Interest Scenario:** Imagine you are a senior executive at a pharmaceutical company. You discover that a close family member is heavily invested in a startup your company is considering for a partnership. The partnership could be highly profitable, but your connection could be viewed as a conflict of interest. Navigate the scenario to address the conflict of interest without harming your family relations or your company's interests.
- **Resource Allocation in Scarcity Scenario:** You are the head of a hospital during a severe flu outbreak, and there is a limited supply of a life-saving drug. It would be best if you decided how to allocate the doses among more potential patients than the doses can cover. Make allocation decisions that consider both medical ethics and public health priorities.
- **AI and Data Privacy Scenario:** You lead a tech company that uses AI to offer personalized shopping experiences. Recent data breaches in the industry have raised concerns about user data privacy. You must decide whether to advance your AI capabilities at the risk of potentially infringing on user privacy. Balance the technological

advancements with ethical considerations regarding user data.

Analysis and Reflection: After participating in each scenario, leaders engage in a structured debriefing session designed to enhance their ethical decision-making:

- **Decision-Making Process Analysis:** Analyze the thought process and ethical reasoning used to make decisions in each scenario. Did you lean more towards utilitarian outcomes, adhere strictly to deontological principles, or use another ethical framework? Reflect on how different decisions could lead to different outcomes and how each aligns with personal and organizational ethical standards.
- **Ethical Framework Application:** Evaluate how effectively you applied the ethical frameworks discussed earlier in the chapter. Which frameworks were most helpful? Were there frameworks that conflicted with each other? Identify areas for improvement in applying these frameworks to complex ethical dilemmas.
- **Outcome Reflection:** Consider the short-term and long-term consequences of the decisions made during the role-plays. Reflect on the impacts on all stakeholders, including potential

benefits and harms. Discuss what was learned from each scenario and how these lessons can be applied to real-world ethical challenges in the leaders' roles.

This chapter aims to significantly enhance leaders' abilities to navigate ethical dilemmas with confidence and integrity by providing practical, scenario-based training and reflective analysis. This practical approach ensures that ethical considerations are deeply integrated into the decision-making process, reinforcing a culture of ethical consciousness within organizations.

As we conclude our exploration of ethical decision-making in this Chapter, it is clear that navigating complex ethical dilemmas is not just a skill but a foundational aspect of effective leadership. This chapter thoroughly examines the philosophical underpinnings of ethics, practical frameworks for ethical decision-making, and the vital role of ethical considerations in corporate governance. The role-playing scenarios show how these concepts apply in real-world situations, challenging leaders to think critically and act with integrity. Leaders must continue fostering a culture of ethical awareness and integrity within their organizations. By consistently applying the ethical frameworks and principles discussed, leaders can ensure that their decisions drive business success, contribute positively to the broader community, and reflect well on their personal and organizational moral standings. Ethical leadership is not merely about avoiding wrongdoing but actively doing right by all stakeholders, thereby cultivating trust, respect, and loyalty crucial for long-term success.

6 Team Decisions

"None of us is as smart as all of us." —Ken Blanchard.

The remarkable saga of NASA's Apollo 13 mission is a profound testament to the strength and necessity of effective team decision-making, especially under severe stress and uncertainty. In April 1970, when an oxygen tank exploded aboard their spacecraft 200,000 miles from Earth, the Apollo 13 crew faced life-threatening conditions. The situation demanded immediate, innovative, and cohesive action.

NASA ground control and the astronauts onboard Apollo 13 displayed an exemplary model of collective intelligence. With limited resources and time, they had to make decisions requiring technical expertise and creative thinking. This situation underscores the pivotal role of communication and collaboration in team decision-making.

- **Emergency Problem-Solving:** The ground team quickly assessed the available resources on the spacecraft and communicated their ideas with the astronauts, demonstrating effective cross-disciplinary teamwork.
- **Creative Solutions:** One of the most critical challenges was adapting the lunar module into a

makeshift "lifeboat" to support life until the crew could return to Earth. This required repurposing the limited resources available, such as modifying the carbon dioxide removal system, which was not designed to support the whole crew for an extended duration.

The Apollo 13 incident illustrated the ability to think critically under pressure and the importance of trust and interdependence among team members. Each decision made by the Apollo 13 team resulted from intense deliberations, simulations, and trust in the collective expertise of the astronauts and the NASA support team.

- **Leveraging Diverse Skills:** The team members' diverse expertise, from engineers to astronauts, was pivotal. Their ability to integrate disparate pieces of information into a coherent plan of action was crucial.
- **Decisive Leadership and Clear Roles:** Effective leadership from mission control, clear communication of roles, and the astronauts' trust in their Earth-based team's decisions were critical. Leadership in such scenarios involves guiding the team through structured problem-solving processes while also being open to innovative ideas from any team member.

The lessons from Apollo 13 extend far beyond aerospace; they resonate deeply with business leaders today who must often make rapid decisions with long-lasting impacts under pressure. This historic event illustrates that the keys to successful team decision-making include:

- **Structured yet Flexible Decision Processes:** Having a structured process for emergency decision-making while remaining flexible enough to adapt to changing situations.
- **Effective Communication:** Ensuring all team members communicate their insights and concerns clearly and immediately.
- **Trust and Unity:** Building a team environment where members trust their colleagues' capabilities and intentions.

Reflecting on the Apollo 13 mission allows this chapter to honor a significant historical event and draw essential lessons applicable to modern team decision-making dynamics. Moving forward, we will explore in-depth aspects of team dynamics, address diversity and inclusion challenges within teams, and provide practical strategies to improve decision-making efficacy.

6.1 GROUP FACILITATION

Effective group decision-making transcends the simple act of assembling a team; it requires a deep understanding and adept management of the dynamics that shape group decision-making processes. This section explores how these dynamics can facilitate or hinder effective team decisions and offers strategies to optimize group interaction.

Understanding Group Dynamics

- **The Impact of Groupthink:** Groupthink occurs when a group's overriding priority is harmony and coherence, often at the expense of making the best decisions. This psychological phenomenon can lead to poor or irrational outcomes as members suppress dissenting viewpoints, fail to analyze options or ignore potential risks critically. To combat groupthink, fostering an environment where dissent is encouraged and valued is essential. Leaders can appoint a "devil's advocate" to challenge group consensus and explore alternative viewpoints intentionally. Regularly rotating this role can prevent anyone from being typecast as the perennial contrarian, thus maintaining the group's balance and openness.
- **Promoting Healthy Conflict:** Healthy conflict involves open and respectful disagreement to explore and evaluate diverse ideas and perspectives. This can lead to more robust

decision-making as the group considers a broader range of information and solutions. The Delphi method is beneficial in facilitating constructive conflict. It involves gathering experts' opinions through questionnaires, with feedback shared anonymously between rounds. This method helps minimize confrontation while encouraging independent and creative thinking, gradually building consensus through informed agreement.

Best Practices for Facilitation

- **Role Assignments and Decision Criteria:** Assigning clear roles and responsibilities within the group helps streamline the decision-making process and ensures that all necessary functions are covered. For instance, having a designated facilitator, note-taker, and timekeeper can keep meetings organized and focused. Setting clear criteria for decision-making at the outset provides a framework that guides the group's discussions and choices. All members should agree upon these criteria to ensure collective buy-in.
- **Encouraging Open Communication:** The physical and psychological environment can significantly impact group dynamics. Ensuring a comfortable and distraction-free setting promotes better engagement and participation. Techniques

such as brainstorming sessions allow for the free flow of ideas and discourage premature judgments. Role-play and structured debates can also be employed to explore different scenarios and viewpoints, enriching the group's understanding and evaluation of the issues.

Leaders can significantly enhance the quality of team decisions by understanding and managing group dynamics effectively. This section provides a comprehensive guide to navigating the complexities of group facilitation, ensuring that teams are effective in their deliberations and inclusive and innovative in their approach to decision-making.

6.2 Team Challenges

While diverse teams can significantly enhance decision-making quality by bringing various perspectives to the table, managing these teams presents unique challenges that must be addressed to fully harness their potential.

Importance of Diversity and Inclusion

- **Enhancing Decision Quality with Diversity:** Diverse teams combine a wide range of experiences and viewpoints, which can lead to more thorough analyses and innovative solutions. Studies indicate that diverse teams are better at problem-solving as they bring non-homogeneous ways of thinking that challenge the status quo and lead to innovative thinking. Research by McKinsey & Company has shown that companies with more diverse workforces perform better financially. Teams that are diverse in ethnicity and gender are more likely to be successful because they can draw from a broader pool of experiences and insights, which is crucial when making complex decisions.

- **Benefits Beyond Performance:** Diverse teams are more adaptable to changing environments. Their wide array of skills and experiences equips them to handle various situations, making the organization more flexible and resilient in the face of change. Teams that are inclusive and respect diverse viewpoints tend to have higher levels of team engagement and satisfaction. This positive work environment often leads to lower turnover rates and higher employee morale.

Challenges in Team Composition

- **Potential Conflicts and Miscommunications:** Differences in cultural backgrounds can lead to misunderstandings and conflicts if not correctly managed. These may stem from differing communication styles, norms, work processes, or behavior expectations. Unconscious biases can undermine the integration of diverse team members and can lead to decisions that are not fully inclusive, potentially marginalizing certain group members and their contributions.

- **Strategies for Overcoming Challenges:** Training that enhances cultural awareness and competence can better prepare team members to understand and integrate diverse perspectives. This training helps recognize and overcome personal biases and develop communication skills across cultures.
- **Inclusive Leadership Practices:** Leaders play a crucial role in modeling inclusive behaviors. Inclusive leadership involves being aware of team members' diverse needs and perspectives, fostering an open and respectful team culture, and ensuring that all voices are heard during decision-making.
- **Conflict Management Mechanisms:** Establishing clear protocols for managing and resolving team conflicts is essential. This might include regular team-building activities that

enhance mutual understanding and formal mediation processes when necessary.

By addressing both the benefits and challenges of diversity in teams, leaders can better prepare to harness the full potential of their diverse workforces. Effectively managing these dynamics enhances decision-making and builds a more innovative, inclusive, and productive organizational culture.

6.3 Diversity Leverage

Leveraging diversity effectively within teams is not just about assembling a diverse workforce; it's about actively engaging and utilizing that diversity to enhance group dynamics and decision-making effectiveness. This section explores practical exercises and structured decision-making processes that can help maximize the benefits of diverse teams.

Exercises to Improve Group Dynamics

- **Scenario Planning:** Scenario planning involves team members working together to develop and analyze possible future scenarios that could impact the organization. This exercise helps teams understand different perspectives and consider various outcomes, which can lead to more robust and creative decision-making. Divide the team into small groups and assign each group a different scenario to develop, focusing on how different variables could affect future outcomes. Afterward, groups present their scenarios and discuss the implications with the broader team. This enhances strategic thinking and fosters a more profound understanding among team members of different viewpoints and considerations.

- **Perspective-Taking Activities:** Perspective-taking exercises build empathy and understanding within teams. These activities encourage members to share their personal experiences and viewpoints, thereby broadening each member's appreciation for different backgrounds and life experiences. Organize sessions where team members can share stories about their cultural background, professional experiences, or personal challenges. This can be structured through storytelling workshops or informal 'get to know' sessions, which help humanize team interactions and reduce biases.

Enhancing Decision-Making Effectiveness

- **Multivoting Systems:** Multivoting is a technique used to narrow down a list of options or decisions by allowing team members to vote on their preferred choices. This method ensures that all team members can contribute to the decision-making process, making it more democratic and inclusive. Present the team with a list of options and give each member a set number of votes they can distribute among the options. The options with the most votes are considered further or finalized depending on the context of the decision.

- **Consensus Decision-Making:** Consensus decision-making seeks all team members' agreement before deciding. It emphasizes discussion and collaboration, ensuring that all opinions are considered and the team collectively supports the final decision. Implement a process where decisions are not finalized until all team members agree. This might involve several rounds of discussion and modification of proposals to address concerns raised by team members. While this process can be time-consuming, it often results in a more substantial commitment to the final decision and better outcomes.

By implementing these exercises and decision-making frameworks, teams can improve their internal dynamics and significantly enhance their problem-solving and decision-making capabilities. Leveraging the full spectrum of diversity within teams leads to more innovative and effective solutions and promotes a more inclusive and harmonious work environment.

As we conclude our exploration of team decisions, it's evident that a team's true strength lies not only in its composite skills but in how effectively it harnesses and leverages the diversity of its members. Through the exercises and strategies discussed in this chapter, leaders are equipped to improve group dynamics, promote inclusivity, and enhance decision-making processes within their teams. Implementing these practices will drive better outcomes and foster a culture of collaboration and respect, which is essential for any team facing the complex challenges of today's business environment. By continuously refining these processes and encouraging open, empathetic communication, organizations can ensure that their teams are not just groups of individuals working together but cohesive units that embody the collective intelligence and creativity necessary to succeed in a competitive landscape.

7 DECISION SPEED

"In any moment of decision, the best thing you can do is the right thing, the next best thing is the wrong thing, and the worst thing you can do is nothing." —Theodore Roosevelt.

This poignant observation by Theodore Roosevelt captures the essence of decision-making, especially in high-stakes situations. It speaks to the inevitable pressure of making uncertain choices, emphasizing that taking action, even if imperfect, is often more beneficial than inaction. This principle becomes particularly critical during crises, where the timeliness of decisions can drastically influence outcomes.

The 2008 financial crisis is a prime example of the importance of swift decision-making. Quick and decisive actions were essential as financial institutions teetered on the brink of collapse and the global economy faced unprecedented disruption. Governments and central banks worldwide responded by implementing emergency bailouts and adjusting monetary policies. These measures, although controversial, were crucial in stabilizing the financial system and mitigating the potential for a deeper economic downturn. For instance, the Troubled Asset Relief Program (TARP) in the United States restored confidence in the financial markets by providing the banks with the capital needed to continue operations.

These rapid responses underscored a dual challenge leaders often encounter during crises: balancing speed with accuracy. On the one hand, quick decision-making can prevent further crisis escalation, limit damage, and capitalize on narrow windows of opportunity. On the other hand, the pressure to act quickly can lead to oversights, errors in judgment, or actions based on incomplete information, potentially leading to long-term negative consequences.

The complexity of this balance is not limited to financial crises. Leaders in all sectors may face similar pressures, whether dealing with a corporate emergency, a public health crisis, or urgent environmental issues. The ability to navigate this balance effectively can be the difference between a successful resolution and a disastrous outcome. It involves the capacity to assess situations rapidly and act decisively and the foresight to anticipate the potential impacts of those decisions.

Therefore, understanding and improving the speed of decision-making is crucial for leaders. This chapter explores how leaders can develop strategies to enhance their decision-making speed without compromising the thoroughness and accuracy needed to make effective decisions. By examining historical and contemporary examples, like the 2008 financial crisis, leaders can glean insights into the dynamics of rapid decision-making and apply these lessons to their contexts.

7.1 SPEED BALANCE

In the dynamic realm of business, the ability to make decisions quickly can often be as critical as the decisions themselves. Influential leaders must find ways to accelerate decision-making processes without compromising the accuracy and integrity of those decisions.

- **Optimized Communication Channels:** Organizations can optimize communication channels by removing unnecessary bureaucratic layers to minimize delays. For example, implementing a flat organizational structure where decision-makers are more accessible can reduce the time spent on approvals and increase the organization's responsiveness.
- **Leveraging Technology:** Advanced technologies like AI for predictive analytics can foresee issues and provide solutions faster than traditional methods. Machine learning algorithms can analyze past decision outcomes and streamline current processes by predicting the

most effective approaches. Tools like ERP systems integrate data across departments, providing a holistic view that can speed up decision relevance and accuracy.

- **Establishing Clear Guidelines:** Develop standardized criteria that can be universally applied across similar decision-making scenarios. This speeds up the process and maintains consistency in decision quality, reducing outcome variability.
- **Automation of Routine Decisions:** Automate routine decision-making where possible. For example, set up automated workflows for standard procurement decisions, where purchases below a specific budget are automatically approved if they meet set criteria.
- **Satisficing in Action:** In fast-paced environments, like stock trading or emergency response, the speed of decision-making can be critical. Here, satisficing enables decision-makers to act quickly on the best available information without waiting for the perfect option, which may come too late.
- **Training for Intuition:** Leaders can improve their intuitive decision-making skills, which supports satisfaction by allowing them to make

confident, quick decisions based on their experience and the information at hand.

- **High Frequency, Low Impact:** Identify decision areas that are high frequency but low impact, where quick decisions can be made routinely without extensive deliberation. For instance, daily operational decisions in a manufacturing line about minor adjustments to production can be made quickly based on predefined standards or past experiences.

- **Use of Decision Matrices:** Implement decision matrices that classify decisions based on their impact and urgency. This helps quickly identify which decisions need immediate action and which can be deliberated more extensively.

- **Regular Drills and Simulations:** Conduct regular drills and simulations to practice quick decision-making scenarios. This helps refine the decision-making process under pressure and builds confidence among team members in their ability to handle real situations effectively.

- **Feedback Loops:** Establish quick feedback loops that provide immediate insights into decision outcomes. This rapid feedback helps correct course if needed and reinforces the learning from each decision-making instance.

Thus, by incorporating the strategies outlined above, leaders can effectively enhance the speed of their decision-making processes without compromising decision quality or results. Maintaining this delicate balance is essential for ensuring agility and sustaining a competitive advantage in a rapidly evolving market.

7.2 QUICK DECISIONS

Rapid and effective decision-making is essential, particularly in environments where conditions change swiftly, and delay can lead to missed opportunities or heightened risks. However, making decisions quickly does not mean rushing through them without due consideration. This section explores optimizing the decision-making process for speed while safeguarding against potential downsides such as decision fatigue and paralysis.

Decision fatigue refers to the deteriorating quality of decisions an individual makes after a lengthy decision-making session. Making decisions is cognitively demanding, and prolonged decision-making can deplete the brain's energy, leading to suboptimal choices. For leaders, decision fatigue can result in procrastination, simplistic decision-making, or even defaulting to the most straightforward choice rather than the best choice. This can be particularly detrimental in high-stakes business environments where strategic decisions need sharp acuity.

Offloading decisions to trusted team members can help leaders manage their cognitive load. Delegation reduces the number of decisions leaders must make and empowers team members by entrusting them with more responsibilities.

- **Decision Prioritization:** Not all decisions require the same level of detailed attention. Prioritizing decisions based on their impact and urgency can help leaders focus their energy and cognitive resources on truly significant choices.
- **Scheduled Breaks:** Incorporating planned breaks into decision-making can help refresh mental resources. Even short breaks can provide a mental reset that helps maintain decision-making clarity and prevent fatigue.

Techniques to Enhance Quick Decision-Making: The OODA Loop

Military strategist Colonel John Boyd developed the OODA Loop for Observe, Orient, Decide, and Act. It is a decision cycle that emphasizes speed and agility. Initially used in combat operations, it is now applied in various fields, including business. The OODA Loop encourages rapid collection and processing of information (Observe), understanding the situation and the context (Orient), making a decision (Decide), and taking action (Act). Leaders can make faster, more responsive decisions by continuously cycling through these steps.

- **Rapid Observation:** Gather the most recent and relevant data to inform your decision. This may involve real-time data feeds, quick updates from team members, or automated alerts.
- **Swift Orientation:** Analyze the data in the context of your objectives and the overall environment. This requires a clear understanding of both the external environment and internal capabilities.
- **Decisive Action:** Based on the current information, Choose the best course of action and execute it. The key is to make the decision quickly and adapt as more information becomes available.
- **Continuous Feedback:** After acting, immediately gather feedback on the effects of your decision. This feedback will inform your next observation phase, allowing quick adjustments and improvements.

By understanding how to effectively manage decision fatigue and employing techniques like the OODA Loop, leaders can enhance their ability to make quick, informed decisions necessary for success in dynamic and high-pressure environments. This approach improves the speed of decision-making and ensures that decisions are thoughtful and grounded in the latest available information.

7.3 AVOIDING PARALYSIS

Analysis paralysis is a common pitfall in decision-making. The fear of making an incorrect decision leads to excessive deliberation and data gathering. This often results in a decision-making process that needs to be improved or significantly slowed, with opportunities potentially being missed.

Signs of Analysis Paralysis:

- **Indecisiveness**: Continuously questioning whether enough information has been gathered or if every possible scenario has been considered.
- **Constant Need for More Data:** Feeling that no data is sufficient leads to perpetual research and consultations without moving toward a decision.
- **Fear of Failure:** Overemphasizing the consequences of making the wrong decision magnifies the risk and leads to hesitation and inaction.

Strategies to Overcome Analysis Paralysis:

- **Set Decision Deadlines:** Implementing strict timelines for decision-making can help compel action and focus the decision-making process.
- **Limit Information Intake:** Define in advance what critical information is necessary to decide and resist the urge to go beyond these parameters unless new, critical information comes to light.
- **Simplify the Process:** Break down complex decisions into smaller, manageable parts. Making decisions on these smaller segments can reduce the pressure and make the overall process more approachable.
- **Accept Imperfection:** Recognize that no decision comes with absolute certainty and that waiting for the perfect solution is often impractical.

Practice Drills to Improve Decision Speed: Practice drills can be highly beneficial for effectively countering analysis paralysis and improving decision-making speed, especially under pressure.

- **Scenario-Based Drills:** Create scenarios that mirror real-world high-stress situations requiring quick decisions. These might simulate emergency business situations, such as a sudden drop in stock prices, a PR crisis, or urgent product recalls. Involve team members in these simulations to role-play different stakeholders. This adds realism and helps leaders practice navigating complex interpersonal dynamics under pressure.

- **Games that Encourage Quick Thinking:** Use games and exercises to foster quick strategic thinking and decision-making. Examples include strategy video games, chess with a timer, or business case competitions conducted under time constraints.

- **Reflection and Feedback:** After each drill or game, conduct a debriefing session to reflect on the decision-making process, discussing what was effective, what wasn't, and how decision-making could be improved in future scenarios.

- **Incremental Decision Practice**: Begin with low-stakes decisions to build confidence and competence. Gradually increase the complexity and stakes of the decisions in practice drills to better prepare for real-life high-stakes situations. Use feedback from each session to refine decision-making skills. This continuous loop of action, feedback, and adjustment is crucial for developing proficiency in making quick, effective decisions.

By understanding and addressing analysis paralysis and through targeted practice drills, leaders can enhance their ability to make prompt, effective decisions. This boosts their confidence in their decision-making abilities and ensures that their organizations can thrive in dynamic and potentially volatile environments.

As we conclude our exploration of decision speed in this chapter, we recognize the delicate balance between acting swiftly and maintaining decision accuracy. This chapter has underscored the importance of addressing and mitigating decision fatigue, avoiding analysis paralysis, and enhancing our decision-making processes through practical drills and strategies. Leaders who master the art of quick decision-making without sacrificing quality will empower their organizations to navigate crises effectively, seize opportunities promptly, and maintain a competitive edge in the fast-paced modern marketplace. Ultimately, the ability to make timely decisions under pressure is not just a skill but a critical leadership asset that drives organizational success and resilience.

8 COMMUNICATING DECISIONS

"The art of communication is the language of leadership."
—James Humes.

Effective communication is not just a supplementary skill for leaders; it is central to effective leadership and executing strategic decisions. How leaders communicate decisions can significantly influence their acceptance and implementation, affecting everything from team morale to public perception and stakeholder engagement.

Take the case of Tim Cook, CEO of Apple, who announced the company's initiative to enhance its environmental sustainability significantly. Cook's approach was exemplary in its clarity and thoroughness, providing detailed insights into the initiative's goals and the steps Apple would take to achieve them. By articulating the decision in a way that highlighted both ethical considerations and long-term corporate benefits, Cook was able to secure broad support across diverse stakeholder groups, from Apple employees and customers to investors and environmental organizations.

In stark contrast, consider an incident involving a major airline where a passenger was forcibly removed from an overbooked flight. The airline's initial communications were vague and defensive, lacking empathy for the affected passenger and failing to explain the circumstances leading to the decision adequately. The result was a public relations disaster that escalated into a global outcry, severely damaging the airline's reputation and eroding trust among customers and the general public.

These examples underscore the profound impact of communication styles and strategies on the outcome of critical decisions. How decisions are conveyed dramatically alters stakeholders' reactions, potentially changing a supportive consensus into widespread dissent.

- **Internal vs. External Communication:** The Apple example also highlights the importance of aligning internal and external communication strategies. While stakeholders inside and outside the organization may have different perspectives and interests, consistent, transparent communication ensures that all parties are adequately informed and can see the rationale behind decisions.
- **Crisis Communication:** The airline incident is a cautionary tale about the importance of preparedness in crisis communication. Effective communication during a crisis involves addressing the immediate issue and managing the

broader impact on the organization's reputation and stakeholder trust.

This chapter will explore various aspects of decision communication, focusing on techniques that enhance clarity, ensure consistency, and foster an environment of transparency and trust. Leaders will learn how to effectively communicate complex decisions, handle resistance gracefully, and maintain open lines of communication that reinforce their leadership and facilitate the successful implementation of decisions.

This chapter delves into the nuances of communicating decisions. It aims to equip leaders with the necessary tools to make wise decisions and articulate them effectively to all stakeholders, enhancing their leadership's overall impact and effectiveness.

8.1 DECISION COMMUNICATION

Effective decision-making communication is a critical skill for leaders, impacting everything from day-to-day operations to strategic initiatives. Let us explore practical frameworks and adaptive strategies to ensure that decision-making communication is clear, targeted, and practical, facilitating better understanding and engagement across all levels of an organization.

Situation-Background-Assessment-Recommendation (SBAR): Originally developed within the healthcare industry to improve urgent communication, the SBAR framework provides a simple and effective structure for communicating complex information quickly and clearly. It breaks down communication into four components:

- **Situation:** Clearly and briefly define the current situation or problem.
- **Background:** Provide the necessary background information directly related to the situation.
- **Assessment:** Share an analysis of the developments that have led to the current state.
- **Recommendation:** Suggest a course of action or decision to be taken.

SBAR can be particularly effective in business settings where decisions must be communicated across different departments or levels of management. It ensures that all parties understand what is happening, why it is essential, and what needs to be done.

The Pyramid Principle: Developed by Barbara Minto at McKinsey & Company, the Pyramid Principle is a communication tool that helps structure points logically, starting with the conclusion.

- **Start with the Conclusion:** Begin communication with the outcome or decision.
- **Supporting Arguments:** Follow with grouped arguments that support the conclusion in a hierarchical structure.
- **Evidence and Data:** End with data and evidence that underpin these arguments.

This method is excellent for ensuring that communications are concise and impactful. It focuses first on the decision and then on why it is logical, necessary, and data-supported. This is particularly effective for written communications like reports or email updates.

The PREP Method: Point, Reason, Example, Point (PREP) is another structured approach to communication that ensures messages are well-rounded and persuasive.

- Point: State your decision or the point you are communicating.
- Reason: Explain why this decision or the point is valid.
- Example: Provide examples or evidence that support your reasoning.
- Point: Reiterate the point at the end to reinforce the message.

PREP is particularly useful in presentations or discussions where a decision needs to be justified or sold to the team or stakeholders. It ensures that the communication is balanced between assertion and evidence.

Adaptive Strategies for Different Stakeholders: Understanding the needs of different stakeholders and tailoring communications accordingly is crucial.

- **Segmentation:** Identify different groups affected by the decision based on their stakes and needs.
- **Customization:** Customize the message for each segment, addressing specific concerns and how the decision impacts them.
- **Feedback Mechanisms:** Establish channels for stakeholders to provide feedback, which can help refine future communications and decisions.

Adaptive communication requires leaders to be versatile in presenting decisions to different audiences. For instance, technical details may be crucial when communicating with IT teams, whereas strategic impacts might be more relevant to executive stakeholders.

Feedback and Continuous Improvement: Implementing a feedback loop is vital for refining decision-making communication.

- **Collect Feedback:** Regularly solicit feedback on how decisions are communicated.
- **Analyze Feedback:** Analyze the feedback to identify areas for improvement.
- **Implement Changes**: Make necessary adjustments to improve clarity and effectiveness.

Continuous improvement in communication should be a priority. This could be facilitated through surveys, direct feedback sessions, or even informal conversations post-communication.

By applying these communication frameworks and adapting messages to meet the specific needs of different stakeholders, leaders can enhance the effectiveness of their decision communications. This ensures that decisions are understood, well-received, supported, and effectively implemented, aligning with the organization's strategic goals.

8.2 Handling Resistance

Resistance to decisions is a common challenge in leadership and management, particularly when significant changes impact well-established procedures or benefits. Understanding and effectively managing this resistance is crucial for ensuring smooth implementation and minimizing disruption.

Sources of Resistance

- **Fear of Change:** Change can be intimidating, especially if it threatens the status quo or individuals' comfort zones. This fear can manifest as resistance, mainly if the outcomes of the change are uncertain or perceived as potentially damaging.
- **Misunderstandings:** Resistance often arises from misunderstandings about the nature of the decision or its implications. If stakeholders do not clearly understand why a decision was made or believe misinformation about its effects, they may resist based on these misconceptions.
- **Differing Assessments:** Individuals may have different perspectives or information that lead them to assess the situation differently. They might disagree if their data or analysis suggests a better alternative.

Strategies for Managing Resistance

- **Engaging Directly with Resistant Parties:** Direct engagement involves having open dialogues with those who resist a decision. This can include one-on-one meetings, roundtable discussions, or informal chats. The goal is to understand their concerns and provide a forum to voice them.

- **Offering Reassurances:** It is essential to address stakeholders' concerns by reassuring them about the decision's benefits and the measures taken to mitigate any negative impacts. This might include detailing support structures put in place to help them adapt to the change or how the decision ultimately aligns with the long-term goals that benefit all.

- **Providing Clear Explanations:** Communicating the rationale behind a decision clearly and transparently can alleviate fears and build trust. Explain the decision-making process, the data or evidence used to reach the decision, and why this option was chosen. This clarity can help stakeholders understand the decision better and reduce resistance based on misconceptions.

- **Using Empathetic Communication:** Approach all communications with empathy. Recognize and acknowledge the feelings and concerns of those affected by the decision. Demonstrating understanding and compassion can help lower resistance and foster a more cooperative atmosphere.

- **Seeking Feedback:** Encourage stakeholders to provide feedback on the decision and its implementation. This gives them a sense of involvement and control and provides valuable insights that can be used to adjust strategies or correct misunderstandings. Feedback mechanisms can include surveys, suggestion boxes, or interactive Q&A sessions.
- **Facilitating Adaptation:** Help stakeholders adapt to the decision by providing training, resources, or modifications based on feedback. Show flexibility where possible to accommodate reasonable concerns, which can decrease resistance and increase buy-in.

By understanding the sources of resistance and implementing these strategic approaches, leaders can facilitate smoother transitions and more successful decision-making. Effective resistance management improves the immediate outcomes of a decision and strengthens the organization's overall health and resilience by fostering a culture of openness, trust, and adaptability.

8.3 Transparency Role

Transparency is a cornerstone of effective leadership and is particularly crucial in decision-making. Being transparent means more than just communicating decisions clearly—it involves openly sharing the thought processes, data, and considerations that lead to those decisions.

- **Importance of Transparency:** Transparency helps build and maintain trust with stakeholders by showing that decisions are made fairly and based on sound reasoning. It demonstrates respect for the team and stakeholders by valuing their understanding and involvement. Leaders who consistently share transparent and honest information about their decisions are seen as more credible and reliable. This credibility is essential during change or crisis when stakeholder buy-in is critical.
- **Facilitating Better Understanding:** When stakeholders understand the reasons behind decisions, they are more likely to support them, even if the outcomes are not immediately beneficial or favorable. Transparency helps stakeholders see the big picture and understand how specific decisions fit broader organizational goals. Openness in decision-making invites feedback, which can provide insights that might not have been considered initially. This feedback loop can lead to improved decisions in the future.

Tips for Maintaining Transparency

- **Regular Updates and Communication:** Keep stakeholders informed throughout the decision-making process, not just about the final decision. Regular updates about the stages of decision-making, the factors being considered, and any changes in direction are crucial for maintaining transparency. Use multiple channels to communicate updates and decisions to reach different segments of your audience effectively. This might include emails, intranet posts, meetings, and briefings.
- **Holding Q&A Sessions:** Schedule regular question-and-answer sessions where stakeholders can ask questions directly to the decision-makers. This allows for real-time clarification of doubts and demonstrates the leadership's commitment to transparency. Ensure those involved in decision-making are prepared to answer questions comprehensively and honestly, reinforcing a culture of openness.
- **Detailed Background Sharing:** Provide detailed background information on the decisions, including the data used, the alternatives considered, the pros and cons of each, and why a particular course of action was

chosen. Maintain records of decision-making processes that can be referenced or audited if necessary. This documentation should be accessible to stakeholders where appropriate.

- **Admitting Provisionally and Uncertainties:** Be upfront about the uncertainties or risks associated with the decision. Admitting that some decisions are provisional and may change as more information becomes available can help maintain trust. Communicate that the leadership is prepared to adjust decisions based on new information or feedback, which can reassure stakeholders that the leadership is responsive and adaptable.

By emphasizing transparency in decision-making, leaders can foster an organizational culture that values openness, encourages engagement, and builds trust. This approach supports the implementation of decisions and strengthens the organization's overall resilience and adaptability.

As we conclude our discussion on communicating decisions, it's evident that the impact of a decision largely depends on its communication. Clear, transparent communication builds trust, enhances understanding, and ensures effective implementation. This chapter has outlined key frameworks for clear messaging, strategies to manage resistance, and the importance of transparency for credibility. Leaders skilled in these areas can ensure their decisions are well-received, enhancing their integrity and effectiveness. Continuously refining these communication skills is vital, as effective communication is essential for sustained leadership success and organizational resilience.

9 Reflecting Decisions

> "We do not learn from experience... we learn from reflecting on experience." —John Dewey.

Reflective practice is an indispensable aspect of effective leadership and decision-making. It allows leaders and organizations to understand the outcomes of their decisions and the underlying dynamics and processes that led to those outcomes. This understanding is pivotal in enhancing future decision-making capabilities.

Take, for example, a major technology company's strategic shift from primarily selling hardware products to offering software services. This bold decision was initially met with considerable skepticism from the market and the company's stakeholders. Critics doubted the feasibility and timing of such a shift, given the company's longstanding identity as a hardware manufacturer. However, this move eventually proved a game-changer, significantly enhancing the company's market position and setting it on a path of rapid growth and profitability.

In-depth Analysis of Strategic Pivot:

- **Retrospective Analysis:** A thorough retrospective analysis of this decision revealed several critical insights. It showed how the company's leadership accurately read the shifting trends in technology consumption and the growing demand for software solutions. This analysis also sheds light on the risk management strategies to mitigate potential setbacks during the transition phase.

- **Learning from Market Analysis:** The decision underscored the importance of in-depth market analysis and its role in shaping strategic pivots. The company could make informed decisions that capitalize on emerging opportunities by understanding customer needs and industry trends.
- **Adaptive Strategies Uncovered:** The analysis highlighted the adaptive strategies crucial for overcoming the challenges during this transition. These included investing in new technologies, restructuring internal processes, and upskilling the workforce to align with the new business model.

Delving into Reflective Practices

In this chapter, we explore the processes and benefits of reflective decision-making. Reflective practice is not just about looking back; it is about learning from the past to inform and improve future actions.

- **Structured Methods for Analysis:** We will introduce structured methods such as decision post-mortems, which involve dissecting decisions after their outcomes are known to understand what went well and what did not. This method helps pinpoint decision-making errors, unforeseen variables, and the validity of underlying assumptions.
- **Cultural Significance:** Reflecting on decisions also has significant cultural implications for an organization. It fosters a learning and continuous improvement culture, shifting the focus from individual blame to collective learning. We will discuss how organizations can cultivate a culture that sees every outcome as an opportunity to learn and grow.
- **Institutionalizing Reflective Practices:** We will provide practical tools and frameworks to help organizations institutionalize these reflective practices. This includes templates for conducting decision reviews, guidelines for setting up feedback loops, and strategies for integrating reflective practices into the organization's daily routines.

By thoroughly analyzing past decisions and institutionalizing these reflective practices, organizations can enhance their strategic agility and resilience, making them better equipped to navigate the complexities and uncertainties of today's business environment. This chapter aims to empower leaders with the knowledge and tools to make decisions and learn effectively from them, thereby fostering a proactive and learning-driven organizational culture.

9.1 Importance of Reflection

Reflective practice is a critical component of effective decision-making. It allows leaders and organizations to systematically analyze successful and unsuccessful decisions, which is fundamental for continuous improvement and strategic refinement.

Teaching Analytical Methods:

- **Systematic Analysis through Decision Post-Mortem:** A decision post-mortem is a thorough review of the decision-making process after the outcomes are known. This structured debrief involves a team coming together to closely examine what happened, pinpointing what worked and what didn't, and exploring the reasons behind these outcomes. The process begins with a detailed recount of the decision timeline, followed by examining the context in which the decision was made, the goals it aimed to achieve, the actions implemented, and the results obtained. The session wraps up by identifying key lessons and formulating recommendations for future decisions. Techniques such as SWOT analysis (examining Strengths, Weaknesses, Opportunities, Threats), root cause analysis to detect fundamental issues, and gathering feedback from stakeholders to gain external insights into the decision's effects are commonly employed in a post-mortem. This method is crucial for uncovering biases, errors in judgment, and unexpected factors influencing the outcome.

- **Identifying Underlying Assumptions and Errors:** Decisions are often based on assumptions that decision-makers may need to be explicitly aware of. Reflecting helps identify these assumptions and examine them to test them against reality. Decision-making errors such as confirmation bias, overconfidence, or groupthink can be identified through reflective practices. Acknowledging these helps in mitigating similar mistakes in the future.

Application in Leadership Training:

- **Enhancing Decision-Making Acumen**: Incorporating modules on reflective practices in leadership training programs can significantly enhance a leader's ability to make informed decisions. Training should include hands-on sessions where leaders practice conducting post-mortems and analyzing real-life decisions within the organization. Through these exercises, leaders develop critical thinking and analytical skills essential for high-quality decision-making. They learn to react to outcomes and understand the processes that lead to those outcomes.

- **Strengthening Organizational Capabilities:** Regular reflection on past decisions strengthens the organization's strategic capabilities by embedding a continuous learning and adaptation cycle. This cyclic process ensures that the organization remains dynamic and can adjust its strategies based on concrete insights gained from past experiences. By valuing and institutionalizing reflective practices, organizations foster a culture that encourages continual learning and open sharing of successes and failures. This culture supports risk-taking and innovation and builds a more resilient organization.
- **Continuous Learning and Improvement:** Reflection should be considered an iterative process of the organizational routine. Leaders should schedule regular intervals to review recent

and older decisions to ensure that lessons are integrated into the organization's practices. Incorporating feedback mechanisms where employees at all levels are encouraged to contribute their insights can further enhance the effectiveness of reflective practices. This inclusivity ensures that diverse perspectives are considered, enriching the learning process.

By understanding the importance of reflection and systematically applying it in leadership training and organizational processes, leaders can transform decision-making from static to dynamic, continually evolving based on past insights and experiences. This not only refines individual leader competencies but also fundamentally strengthens the organization's strategic foundation.

9.2 Analyzing Outcomes

Effective decision-making isn't just about immediate results; it also involves deep analysis of those outcomes to refine and enhance organizational strategies and operations continually. Central to this is the cultivation of a learning culture within the organization.

- **Importance of a Learning Culture:** A learning culture actively encourages the continuous analysis of decisions and outcomes.

This culture is built on transparency and psychological safety principles, enabling employees to share their insights and concerns without fear of reprisal or criticism. Creating an environment where employees feel safe discussing and learning from failures and successes is crucial. This safety encourages open communication and the sharing of ideas, which are essential for innovative thinking and problem-solving.

- **Implementing a Learning Culture:** Schedule regular meetings where teams can discuss the outcomes of recent decisions. These sessions should focus on what went wrong, successful outcomes, and what can be learned from both. Facilitate sessions that involve multiple departments to discuss critical decisions and outcomes. This approach helps break down silos within the organization and fosters a more integrated learning environment.
- **Training and Development:** Invest in training programs that emphasize skills in critical thinking, data analysis, and reflective practices. This training helps embed a culture of learning at the individual level.

Benefits to the Organization

- **Enhanced Decision-Making Skills:** Regularly analyzing decision outcomes helps refine and optimize strategies by identifying what is effective and what needs adjustment. This ongoing refinement is crucial for maintaining relevance and competitiveness in a fast-changing business environment. Continuous feedback and learning from past decisions lead to process improvements. These improvements can reduce inefficiencies, enhance productivity, and ultimately improve outcomes.
- **Organizational Adaptability:** A learning culture fosters an adaptive and flexible workforce capable of responding to changes and challenges more effectively. Employees accustomed to regular analysis and feedback are better prepared to swiftly adjust their strategies and approaches. Organizations that embrace a learning culture tend to be more innovative. Organizations can spark new ideas and approaches that drive innovation by encouraging exploration and discussion of failures and successes.
- **Building Resilience:** A culture that continuously learns from its decisions builds resilience. This resilience manifests as the organization's ability to withstand setbacks and

navigate challenges successfully, learning and growing from each experience.

By fostering a culture that values outcomes analysis and supports continuous learning, organizations enhance their decision-making capabilities and create a more dynamic, responsive, and resilient organization. This learning-oriented approach ensures that the organization remains agile and can thrive in dynamic and sometimes unpredictable business environments.

9.3 CONTINUOUS IMPROVEMENT:

Continuous improvement is an essential strategy for enhancing the decision-making process within organizations. It involves iterative learning and development, which is critical for effectively adapting to new challenges and opportunities. The use of structured templates for decision review sessions and the establishment of robust feedback loops are central to facilitating this continuous improvement.

Templates for Decision Review: Templates provide a standard and structured approach to conducting decision reviews. They help ensure that each session is focused and efficient by outlining specific questions to address, metrics to evaluate, and topics to discuss. Templates ensure consistency in decision reviews across different departments or teams, which is crucial for uniformly comparing results and learning. Templates should include essential questions that provoke thoughtful analysis and insights. Questions might include:

- What were the expected outcomes of the decision?
- What was the reality?
- What were the key factors that influenced the outcome?
- **Metrics for Assessment:** Identify specific metrics or KPIs (Key Performance Indicators) that need to be assessed during the review. Depending on the nature of the decision, these could relate to performance, cost, time, customer satisfaction, etc.
- **Areas for Discussion**: Highlight specific areas for discussion, such as resource allocation, process effectiveness, or stakeholder reactions. This ensures that all relevant aspects of the decision are explored.

Establishing Feedback Loops: Feedback loops facilitate regular collection, analysis, and incorporation of feedback into future decisions. They are vital for learning from experiences and adapting processes or strategies based on that learning. Effective feedback loops allow organizations to make real-time adjustments, enhancing agility and responsiveness. Set up regular intervals for feedback collection, which can be through digital surveys, focus groups, or one-on-one interviews, depending on the depth of feedback needed.

- **Analysis of Feedback:** Analyze the feedback systematically to identify patterns, issues, or opportunities. This analysis should involve qualitative and quantitative methods to understand the feedback comprehensively.
- **Response and Implementation:** Develop a process for responding to feedback and implementing necessary changes. This process should include prioritizing feedback based on its impact and feasibility and assigning responsibilities for implementing changes.
- **Communication Back to Stakeholders**: Ensure that feedback providers see that their input has been considered and acted upon. This closes the feedback loop and encourages ongoing engagement and contribution from stakeholders.

Organizations can foster a culture of continuous improvement by implementing structured decision review templates and establishing robust feedback loops. This culture not only drives better decision-making but also builds an organization that is resilient, adaptive, and capable of sustaining long-term success.

As we conclude this chapter, we emphasize the crucial role of reflection in the decision-making process. Reflecting on decisions facilitates a deeper understanding of successes and failures and fosters an organization's continuous improvement culture. Organizations can enhance their strategic agility and decision-making acuity by systematically employing structured review sessions, integrating effective templates, and establishing dynamic feedback loops. This chapter has equipped leaders with the tools to institutionalize these practices, ensuring that every decision, regardless of its immediate outcome, becomes a stepping stone toward greater organizational wisdom and resilience. As leaders, embracing these reflective practices means committing to an ongoing journey of learning and growth—a commitment that will invariably lead to enhanced performance and sustained organizational success.

10 Decision Skills

"Good decision-making is not a skill you are born with, but one that is sharpened through diligence and practice." —Unknown.

The ability to make sound decisions is not inherent; it is a skill honed through careful and consistent practice. Decision-making is a critical competence in leadership and management and is pivotal to personal and organizational success. This chapter delves deep into developing a personal development plan focused on enhancing your decision-making skills, an essential tool for any professional aiming to excel in leadership roles.

Crafting a Personal Development Plan for Decision-Making: Each individual's decision-making skills and needs vary, so it is crucial to tailor a personal development plan that addresses specific areas of improvement. This plan involves a thorough assessment of current decision-making strengths and weaknesses, setting precise, achievable goals, and outlining detailed steps to reach these goals. A personal development plan for decision-making includes identifying essential skills such as analytical thinking, emotional intelligence, risk assessment, and ethical judgment. It pinpoints learning opportunities and resources to enhance these areas, such as specific courses, books, or experiential learning through real-world practice.

Importance of Personal Initiative and Ongoing Development

- **Personal Initiative:** The drive to improve decision-making must come from within. Personal initiative is critical because it motivates you to pursue learning actively and apply what you learn to practical scenarios. It involves seeking challenges that test your decision-making in safe environments, reflecting on the outcomes, and adjusting strategies accordingly.
- **Ongoing Development:** Decision-making is a dynamic skill set that requires continual refinement and adaptation. The landscapes in which decisions are made are constantly changing, influenced by technological advancements, market shifts, and cultural trends. Ongoing development is crucial to keep your decision-making skills relevant and sharp. This might involve regular reviews and updates to your personal development plan to include new knowledge and tools as they become available.

Application Across Leadership Levels

- **Seasoned Leaders:** For those with extensive experience, enhancing decision-making skills might focus on areas like strategic foresight and mentoring others in their decision-making processes. Their personal development plans may include advanced leadership courses, strategic retreats, or developing white papers that refine and share their expertise.
- **Emerging Managers:** Newer leaders might concentrate on foundational decision-making skills such as problem-solving techniques, effective communication, and essential risk management. Their development plans might include hands-on management training, mentoring from senior leaders, and active participation in decision-making processes in their current roles.

This chapter establishes that decision-making proficiency is a cultivated rather than an innate ability. By adopting a structured approach to personal development, leaders at all levels can enhance their capacity to make informed, effective decisions. This not only elevates their own strategic impact and leadership effectiveness but also significantly contributes to the resilience and success of their organizations.

10.1 Personal Action Plan

Developing a personal action plan for improving decision-making skills is essential for any leader committed to professional growth and effectiveness. This plan serves as a roadmap, guiding the enhancement of decision-making capabilities through structured learning and resource engagement.

Identifying Learning Opportunities:

- **Specialized Courses:** Enrolling in courses that focus on strategic thinking helps leaders develop the ability to see the bigger picture and anticipate potential challenges before they arise. Problem-solving courses enhance one's capacity to tackle issues efficiently as they arise, using systematic methods to analyze and resolve them. Understanding and analyzing risk is fundamental to making informed decisions. Courses focusing on risk analysis teach leaders how to assess and mitigate potential downsides, preparing them to handle uncertainty more effectively.
- **Seminars and Workshops:** Attending seminars and workshops provides opportunities for learning and networking with other professionals who can offer different perspectives and experiences. These events often feature expert speakers who share the latest trends and

methodologies in decision-making, providing attendees with cutting-edge knowledge and skills. Workshops, in particular, offer hands-on experiences where leaders can practice new techniques in a controlled, educational environment. This practical application is crucial for mastering the skills discussed.

Utilizing Resources

- **Building a Comprehensive Resource List**: A well-rounded resource list should include books that provide in-depth exploration of theories and case studies, articles that offer current views and analysis, podcasts that one can listen to during commutes or downtime, and videos that demonstrate techniques or offer seminars in a digestible format. Examples of Key Resources:
    1. Books like Daniel Kahneman's Thinking, Fast and Slow explore how different conditions influence decisions.
    2. Podcasts such as "Choiceology" can expose listeners to real-life decision-making stories and the psychology behind them.
    3. Online platforms like TED Talks provide access to thought leaders and innovators who share insights into their decision-making processes and outcomes.

- **Regularly Updating and Engaging with Resources:** The fields of strategy and decision-making evolve constantly. New theories and technologies emerge that can significantly impact how decisions are made. Regularly updating your resources ensures you know the latest tools and strategies. Having resources alone is not enough. Setting regular schedules to read books, listen to podcasts, and watch relevant programs can help integrate continuous learning into daily routines. Joining book clubs or discussion groups, both in-person and online, can also enhance understanding and retention of the material learned.

By crafting and following a personal action plan, leaders ensure their development in decision-making is progressive and structured. This improves their capabilities and sets a standard within their organizations for approaching growth and learning in decision-making skills.

10.2 Skills Development

Developing decision-making skills is a dynamic process that benefits significantly from direct, personalized guidance through mentoring and coaching. This approach sharpens not only existing skills but also introduces new perspectives and techniques, enhancing the overall strategic acumen of leaders.

Role of Mentors and Coaches

- **Personalized Guidance:** Mentors and coaches provide tailored advice based on their extensive experience and understanding of decision-making challenges. They serve as a valuable resource for discussing strategic issues, exploring solutions, and refining leadership techniques.
- **Learning from Experience:** These relationships allow you to benefit from the lived experiences of seasoned leaders. Mentors and coaches can share anecdotes and examples from their careers, offering insights into how they handled similar situations and what outcomes their decisions produced. This real-life context enriches learning, making theoretical concepts more tangible and applicable.
- **Regular Sessions:** Effective mentoring and coaching relationships are characterized by regular, scheduled interactions allowing ongoing discussion and feedback. These sessions can be structured around current challenges, recent decisions, or specific learning objectives.
- **Goal-Oriented Feedback:** Feedback in these sessions is typically goal-oriented, focusing on

specific developmental areas such as enhancing analytical thinking, improving risk management strategies, or boosting emotional intelligence in decision-making.

Benefits of Experienced Guidance

- **Blind Spots in Decision-Making:** Everyone has blind spots or areas where their reasoning or habitual responses might not be as robust. Mentors and coaches excel at identifying these areas, helping you see aspects of your decision-making process that you might overlook.
- **Strategies for Improvement:** Once these blind spots are identified, mentors and coaches can suggest strategies and exercises to address them, such as scenario planning, role-playing, or reflective journaling.
- **Expanding Thinking Patterns**: Mentors and coaches challenge you to question and expand your usual thinking patterns. This might involve confronting cognitive biases, examining the underpinnings of your intuitive judgments, or exploring new decision-making models.
- **Encouragement to Experiment:** They encourage experimentation with new methods and strategies, providing a safe space to test ideas before implementing them in high-stakes

environments. This can lead to discovering more influential or innovative ways to make decisions.

- **Speeding Up the Learning Curve:** With direct feedback and guided learning, you can accelerate your progress toward mastering complex decision-making skills.
- **Real-World Application:** Mentors and coaches help bridge the gap between theory and practice, ensuring that the skills you develop are theoretically sound and practically viable in your specific professional context.

Incorporating mentoring and coaching into your personal development plan is a powerful way to enhance decision-making capabilities. This guided approach not only speeds up the learning process but also deepens your understanding of leadership and strategic decision-making, ultimately fostering a more nuanced and sophisticated approach to handling the challenges that come with leadership roles.

10.3 LEADERSHIP EXAMPLE

Effective leadership is not just about making decisions; it's about modeling behaviors and practices that encourage and inspire others to improve their skills. In decision-making, how a leader approaches personal development and continuous learning sets a powerful example for the entire team and organization.

Demonstrating Commitment to Personal Development

- **Visible Learning:** As a leader, actively engaging in your professional development, particularly in enhancing decision-making skills, serves as a visible demonstration of commitment to growth. This might involve sharing your learning experiences, discussing books or resources you've found insightful, or engaging in training sessions with your team.
- **Encouraging Open Dialogue:** Foster an environment where decision-making processes are discussed openly, including the successes and failures. This transparency not only demystifies the decision-making process but also shows that it is a skill that can be developed and refined.
- **Inspiring Improvement:** Regularly updating your decision-making tactics and discussing these strategies with your team inspires them to seek learning opportunities. This can create a culture of continuous improvement where team members feel encouraged to enhance their skills.
- **Setting Standards:** Establish high standards for decision-making within your team by

showcasing meticulous and thoughtful decision analysis, preparation, and execution. Your example can help elevate the overall quality of decisions made across your team.

Call to Action for Continuous Improvement

- **Making a Vow:** The chapter concludes with a potent call to action, urging leaders to commit personally to continually enhancing their decision-making capabilities. This commitment is framed as an individual goal and integral to professional responsibilities.
- **Documenting Progress:** Leaders are encouraged to record their progress and set specific, measurable goals for their decision-making skills. This might involve regular self-assessments or seeking feedback from peers and mentors.
- **Driving Organizational Resilience**: By continuously refining decision-making skills, leaders can significantly impact the resilience and success of their organizations. Improved decision-making leads to better strategy execution, more effective risk management, and enhanced ability to seize opportunities.
- **Legacy of Learning:** Committing to your continuous improvement in decision skills sets a

legacy for current and future leaders within the organization. It signals that leadership development is a perpetual journey, essential for both personal and organizational success.

By leading through example and steadfastly committing to continuous improvement, leaders enhance their decision-making abilities and foster an organizational culture that values growth, resilience, and strategic insight. This approach ensures personal leadership growth and cements a foundation for organizational success and longevity.

As we conclude, it's clear that mastering decision-making is a dynamic, ongoing process that requires active engagement and effort. This chapter highlighted the importance of developing a personal action plan, embracing continuous learning through mentoring and coaching, and exemplifying strong leadership. These elements foster personal growth and a culture of strategic decision-making excellence. Leaders who continuously improve their decision-making skills will boost their leadership effectiveness and inspire their teams. Investing in these skills is essential for navigating today's complex business landscape, ensuring that you and your organization emerge more resilient and prosperous.

11 Conclusion

"The essence of strategy is choosing what not to do." — Michael Porter.

As we draw this exploration to a close, we reflect on the profound journey through the art and science of decision-making. This book has traversed the complex terrain of leadership decisions, from the intricacies of psychological biases to the dynamics of group decision-making and the critical importance of reflective practices. In this concluding chapter, we will summarize the key insights that have shaped your understanding of strategic decision-making, revisit the growth journey of a decision-maker, and introduce the next focus of this series to keep you engaged and looking forward to further enhancing your leadership capabilities.

11.1 Key Insights

The essence of decision-making in leadership encompasses a holistic approach, focusing not only on the outcomes but also critically on the processes that lead to these outcomes. This chapter encapsulates the strategic insights gained throughout the book, collectively serving as a blueprint for enhancing leadership through superior decision-making.

1. **Balancing Speed with Accuracy:** One of the primary insights discussed is balancing the speed of decision-making with the need for accuracy. Rapid decisions can be advantageous and sometimes necessary, but they require a structured approach to ensure they do not sacrifice thoroughness. Leaders must develop the ability to assess situations and determine quickly when swift decisions are appropriate and when more deliberation is needed. Tools like decision matrices or frameworks like the OODA loop (Observe, Orient, Decide, Act) can help make efficient yet accurate decisions.

2. **Benefits of a Structured Decision-Making Framework:** Structured decision-making frameworks provide a systematic approach to complex situations, which can significantly enhance the quality and consistency of decisions. Examples such as the SBAR (Situation, Background, Assessment, Recommendation) technique help structure communication and decision-making processes, especially in high-stakes or fast-paced environments. Tailoring these frameworks to fit your organization's unique needs or specific situations can enhance decision-making effectiveness.

3. **Cultivating a Learning and Reflective Culture:** A critical insight is the importance of fostering an organizational learning-oriented culture. This culture promotes ongoing education, reflection, and feedback, which are essential for continuous improvement in decision-making. Regularly scheduled reflective practices such as decision audits, post-mortems, and feedback sessions help identify successes and areas for improvement, ensuring that decision-making processes evolve with changing organizational needs and external environments.
4. **Practical Application:** These insights are not merely academic but are meant to be actively integrated into daily leadership practices. Leaders are encouraged to apply these principles regularly to ensure their decision-making process is reflective and forward-thinking. Implementing these insights in leadership training programs and development initiatives can help cultivate a new generation of leaders adept at making and analyzing decisions.
5. **Enhancing Organizational Performance:** By integrating these insights into practice, leaders can enhance their strategic decision-making capabilities, leading to better organizational performance and competitiveness. These

practices help organizations adapt and respond to changes, improving overall resilience and success.

In conclusion, the insights gleaned from exploring the multifaceted nature of decision-making equip leaders with the knowledge and tools necessary for effective leadership. By embedding these insights into everyday practice, leaders enhance their capabilities and significantly contribute to their organizations' sustained growth and success.

11.2 Decision-Maker Journey

The path of a strategic decision-maker is not static but dynamic and ongoing, marked by continuous learning, adjustment, and personal growth. Throughout this book, we have explored various dimensions of decision-making, equipping you with a robust set of tools and frameworks designed to refine and enhance your decision-making abilities.

1. **Continual Refinement of Skills:** The journey of a strategic decision-maker involves an ongoing commitment to enhancing and refining decision-making skills. This book provides comprehensive methodologies and approaches, such as analytical frameworks, reflective practices, and leadership examples, to be applied and integrated into daily leadership tasks. The ability to adapt and grow in

response to new challenges is crucial. The tools and frameworks discussed are designed to be flexible, allowing you to modify and apply them as the contexts of your decisions change over time.

2. **Application of Learned Skills:** Applying what has been learned to real-world scenarios is essential for cementing these skills. Each chapter has encouraged the practical application of concepts through exercises, case studies, and actionable strategies, helping to transform theoretical knowledge into practical expertise. Continuously seeking feedback on decision outcomes and being willing to adjust your approaches accordingly are vital practices for any strategic decision-maker. This iterative process ensures that your decision-making process remains practical and relevant.

3. **Commitment to Continuous Learning:** The complexities of the modern business environment necessitate a lifelong commitment to learning. As a leader, embracing this mindset is essential for personal and professional development and fostering a culture of growth within your organization. Actively seeking new learning opportunities, such as advanced courses, seminars, or cross-industry conferences, can

provide fresh insights and perspectives that enhance your decision-making capabilities.

4. **Adaptability in Leadership:** The ability to quickly adapt and refine strategies in response to new information and changing circumstances is a hallmark of effective leadership. This book aims to cultivate an adaptive mindset, encouraging forward-thinking and proactive thinking in anticipating and responding to changes. Encouraging strategic flexibility ensures that, as a leader, you are reacting to changes and strategically positioning yourself and your organization to take advantage of new opportunities and mitigate potential risks.

In summing up the decision-maker's journey, this book emphasizes that true mastery in decision-making is achieved through an unwavering commitment to growth, an adaptive approach to challenges, and a continual application of learned skills. By fostering these attributes, you can ensure sustained success and effectiveness as a leader in an increasingly complex and fast-paced world.

As we close this chapter and the book, we reflect on the profound insights and practices shared to enhance your role as a strategic decision-maker. Throughout "Decision Dynamics," we have navigated the complexities of decision-making, providing you with the tools and insights necessary for profound leadership growth. The journey of a decision-maker is perennial and evolving, demanding continuous refinement and adaptation. This book has been designed to be read and used as a guide in your ongoing development as a leader. As you move forward, remember that decision-making is critical to personal success and your organization's success. Embrace the journey ahead with the commitment to continuous improvement, and prepare to meet future challenges with confidence and strategic prowess.

12 Appendices

"Knowledge is of no value unless you put it into practice."
—Anton Chekhov.

This final chapter is a practical extension of the concepts and strategies explored throughout "Decision Dynamics." Here, we consolidate essential tools, exercises, and resources that will assist you in applying the insights gained to your daily leadership practices. This appendix enhances your journey toward becoming a more strategic and effective decision-maker by offering a curated collection of practical exercises, recommended readings, and thorough references.

12.1 Exercises & Tools

Effective decision-making requires not only theoretical knowledge but also practical application. This section provides a comprehensive suite of exercises and tools to help enhance and refine your decision-making skills through active practice and implementation.

- **Scenario Analysis Activities:** Work through hypothetical scenarios within your business environment. The goal is to apply theoretical decision-making models to these scenarios to see how different approaches affect outcomes. You can use these scenarios in team meetings or training sessions to encourage thinking and discussion about various strategic choices and their possible repercussions. They also help develop a proactive approach to potential challenges.

- **Decision-Making Simulations:** Simulations provide a dynamic platform for practicing decision-making in a controlled, risk-free environment. These simulations are designed to mimic real-life decision-making scenarios. They can be digital or role-play-based and should involve multiple outcomes based on the decisions made during the exercise. This helps participants understand the consequences of their choices tangibly.

- **SWOT Analysis Templates:** SWOT analysis is a straightforward tool for assessing the Strengths, Weaknesses, Opportunities, and Threats related to a particular decision or strategy. Templates can guide teams through completing a SWOT analysis, ensuring that all relevant factors are considered. This exercise is beneficial in strategic planning sessions to evaluate the viability of new projects or strategic shifts.

- **Decision Matrices:** Decision matrices help quantify and compare the benefits and drawbacks of different options based on predefined criteria. Downloadable decision matrix templates can be customized for different decisions, such as vendor selection, product development, or investment opportunities. Using these matrices helps standardize decision-making processes and makes the comparisons more objective.

- **Risk Assessment Frameworks:** These frameworks are essential for identifying and evaluating the potential risks associated with various decisions. They help determine the likelihood and impact of risks, aiding in making more informed decisions. The provided frameworks can include templates for risk identification, risk probability and impact scoring sheets, and mitigation planning. These tools are invaluable in project management and strategic planning, ensuring that all potential risks are systematically assessed and addressed.
- **Feedback Forms:** Feedback forms are critical for gathering input from various stakeholders about the effectiveness of certain decisions or the decision-making process. Customizable feedback forms can be used post-decision to gather insights from employees, customers, or partners. Analyzing this feedback can provide valuable

lessons and guide future decision-making improvements.

By integrating these exercises and tools into regular practice, you and your teams can refine their decision-making skills and foster a culture of strategic thinking and continuous improvement within your organizations. These practical applications ensure that the theoretical knowledge gained from the book is translated into practical, real-world decision-making capabilities.

12.2 RECOMMENDED RESOURCES:

Continued learning and exposure to new ideas are crucial for staying relevant and effective in the rapidly evolving field of leadership and decision-making. This section provides a curated collection of resources to enhance your understanding and application of advanced decision-making theories and practices.

Books:

- "Thinking, Fast and Slow" by Daniel Kahneman – Explores the dual-process theory of the mind and its impact on decision-making.
- "Good Strategy, Bad Strategy" by Richard Rumelt—This book sharply distinguishes between real strategy and mere aspirations, offering a clear

path to creating and implementing a powerful action-oriented strategy for the real world.
- "The Psychology of Persuasion" by Robert Cialdini – A seminal book on understanding the fundamental mechanisms of persuasion and influence, which are critical in decision-making.
- Stanley McChrystal's "Myth and Reality" explores leadership as practiced by various historical and contemporary figures, examining its reality through the lens of differing environments and circumstances.

Articles and Whitepapers: Frequent publications from Harvard Business Review or the "McKinsey Quarterly" offer insightful articles that cover the latest research and trends in strategic decision-making and management practices. Access to journals such as the Journal of Management Studies or Strategic Management Journal provides academic insights into complex decision-making scenarios and the effectiveness of different leadership styles and strategies.

Podcasts:

- **HBR IdeaCast** – A weekly Harvard Business Review podcast featuring leading business and management thinkers.

- **The Decision Corner** – Hosted by Brooke Struck, this podcast explores how insights from behavioral science help us understand and improve decision-making processes.

Video Lectures and Webinars:

- **TED Talks:** Speakers such as Simon Sinek and Dan Gilbert provide accessible and engaging discussions on leadership and psychology that can inform and inspire better decision-making.
- **Webinars:** Many leading business schools and institutions offer free or subscription-based webinars that delve into current challenges and innovations in strategic decision-making. Platforms like Coursera or edX also host lecture series on relevant topics from top universities.
- **Online Courses:** Websites like Udemy, Coursera, and LinkedIn Learning offer interactive courses on decision-making, strategy, and leadership that include practical exercises and community interaction to enhance learning.

These resources are selected for their authoritative content and diversity in perspectives and formats, catering to different learning preferences and needs. By engaging with these recommended books, articles, podcasts, and multimedia materials, you can continue to develop a nuanced understanding of deep and broad decision-making, ensuring readiness to tackle complex decisions with confidence and insight.

12.3 NOTES & REFERENCES

The integrity and value of any academic or professional text are significantly enhanced by its foundations in established research and contributions from the field. This section provides detailed citations and references for the scholarly works, case studies, and articles referenced throughout "Decision Dynamics." Each reference is formatted to include all necessary details, ensuring readers can quickly locate and access these resources for further study.

- Kahneman, Daniel. Thinking, Fast and Slow. Farrar, Straus and Giroux, 2011.
- Rumelt, Richard. Good Strategy Bad Strategy: The Difference and Why It Matters. Crown Business, 2011.
- Smith, John. "Decision Making in Organizational Leadership: A Review," Journal of Business Research, vol. 34,
- "Effective Leadership Practices," Harvard Business Review, accessed March 3, 2022,

- The Decision Corner podcast, hosted by Brooke Struck. Episode 45: "Behavioral Insights on Leadership," aired May 5, 2021.
- Global Leadership Institute, "Innovations in Decision-Making," 2021.
- World Economic Forum, "The Future of Jobs and Skills in Business," 2022.

As we conclude the appendices section of "Decision Dynamics," I hope these resources, references, and acknowledgments serve as valuable tools to further your understanding and application of the principles discussed throughout the book. The exercises and tools provided are designed to enrich your practical skills, while the recommended resources aim to deepen your theoretical knowledge. May this chapter serve as a resource and an inspiration for continuous learning and excellence in your journey as a strategic decision-maker?

Gratitude and Next Steps

As we close the pages of Decision Dynamics, I want to extend my heartfelt thanks to you, the reader, for embarking on this journey through the complex landscape of leadership decision-making. Your commitment to enhancing your strategic decision-making skills is commendable and essential in today's ever-evolving business world.

The journey does not end here. The insights and practices we've explored together are just the beginning. As you continue to apply and refine these strategies, remember that leadership is an ongoing process of learning, adapting, and, most importantly, transforming.

I am excited to announce that the journey continues with the next book in the "Leadership Transformed" series, focusing on "Empathy and Empowerment." This upcoming book will delve into how these critical aspects of leadership can dramatically enhance your effectiveness and influence as a leader. We will explore practical ways to cultivate a deeper understanding of empathy and how to empower those around you, creating a more dynamic, responsive, and compassionate organizational culture.

Stay tuned for a deep dive into empathy and empowerment—key drivers of transformative leadership that inspire and enable teams to achieve their highest potential.

Your engagement and feedback have been invaluable, and I encourage you to stay connected as we prepare for the next installment's release. Please watch our website and subscribe to our newsletter for updates, additional resources, and release dates.

Thank you once again for your commitment to growth and excellence. Let's continue transforming leadership paradigms and creating more empowered and empathetic leadership environments.

Acknowledgments

As I conclude "Decision Dynamics," I am reminded of the vast landscape of knowledge and insight that has influenced the creation of this book. While this journey has primarily been a solitary endeavor, it has been shaped and enriched by the wealth of information and the many thinkers whose works I have had the privilege to access.

I extend my deepest gratitude to the authors, researchers, and thought leaders whose published works have provided foundational knowledge and inspiration for the topics discussed in this book. The countless articles, books, and whitepapers available in the public domain and through various digital platforms have been invaluable. They have informed the content herein and challenged and expanded my perspectives on strategic decision-making.

A special thank you to the online communities and forums for leadership and management. The discussions and debates within these virtual spaces have offered diverse viewpoints and insights that have been critical in shaping my arguments and conclusions.

To my family and friends who have offered encouragement and support throughout this process, your belief in my work has been a source of motivation and resilience. I am profoundly thankful for your patience and understanding as I navigated the complexities of writing this book.

Finally, to readers who engage with this material and seek to enhance your decision-making capabilities, your commitment to growth and excellence is the ultimate inspiration for this work. I hope the strategies and insights offered in "Decision Dynamics" serve you well in your leadership journey.

As we all continue to navigate our paths in leadership and decision-making, may we remain curious, open, and dedicated to pursuing knowledge and understanding? Here's to the ongoing journey of transforming leadership.

ABOUT THE AUTHOR

Dilip Patil has garnered over thirty years of expertise in the information technology sector, navigating governmental and corporate landscapes where he has been recognized for his professional achievements. Beyond his professional success, Dilip adopts a holistic approach to life, valuing personal growth, well-being, and lifelong learning.

Dilip's commitment to maintaining a balance between mind, body, and spirit is exemplified in his role as a devoted yoga instructor and his practice of Ayurvedic life management. These practices underscore his dedication to holistic health and wellness. As an active Toastmasters Club member, he continuously honed his communication and leadership skills, championing the power of effective dialogue and genuine expression.

Born on August 26, 1968, in Pulgaon, a serene village in Maharashtra's Wardha district, Dilip's educational path began at the Hindi-medium Ordinance Factory Higher Secondary School in Katni, Madhya Pradesh. His passion for technology was further nurtured, leading him to earn an Engineering degree from Government Engineering College, Jabalpur, in 1990, followed by a part-time MBA in 2010.

Dilip enjoys a variety of interests, including music, films, motivational literature, and traveling. His dedication to community service, particularly in Nagpur, the vibrant Orange City, highlights his commitment to making a positive societal impact and reflects his belief in transforming challenges into opportunities for growth.

Dilip invites readers to join him on his journey of self-discovery, resilience, and success. Follow him for insights and experiences that light the way to a more fulfilled and intentional life through his social media:

https://www.facebook.com/dilip.patil.3979

https://www.linkedin.com/in/dilip-patil-4066a518

https://www.instagram.com/dilip.patil.3979

Join a community committed to personal development, resilience, and mutual success, fostering an environment of inspiration and continuous growth.

WE VALUE YOUR FEEDBACK

Thank you for exploring "Decision Dynamics: Navigate Complexity, Solve Problems, Cultivate Impact, and Empower Leadership through Strategy." Your journey through the various facets of strategic decision-making is crucial to us, and we are committed to enhancing and refining this resource to better serve leaders like you.

We would greatly appreciate your feedback on this book. Whether it's a particular concept that resonated with you, a chapter that sparked an idea, or suggestions for improvement, we are eager to hear from you. Your insights and experiences are invaluable as they help improve this work and influence the future direction of the "Leadership Transformed" series.

To help us improve and tailor future editions of "Decision Dynamics" and other works in the "Leadership Transformed" series, we would appreciate your responses to the following questions:

- How relevant did you find the content of "Decision Dynamics" to your current leadership and decision-making challenges? Please provide specific examples or areas where the content was particularly applicable.

- What are the top three insights or tools from the book that you found most helpful or impactful in your leadership role?
- Were there any topics or sections in the book that needed deeper exploration or clearer explanations? Please specify.
- How practical were the exercises and tools provided in the book? Are there additional tools or resources in future editions you would like to see included?
- What additional topics or areas of leadership decision-making would you be interested in seeing addressed in future books of the "Leadership Transformed" series?

You can send your thoughts, reviews, and suggestions to **patildilip23@gmail.com**

Your feedback is not just appreciated; it is essential. By sharing your views, you contribute to a larger conversation about leadership and decision-making that extends far beyond the pages of this book. Thank you once again for your commitment to growth and leadership. We look forward to hearing from you and hope to continue providing you with valuable resources that aid your leadership development.

Explore More Titles by Author

Dilip Patil's literary journey extends beyond the transformative insights of "Decision Dynamics: Navigate Complexity, Solve Problems, Cultivate Impact, and Empower Leadership through Strategy" and the "LEADERSHIP TRANSFORMED" series. Through his other esteemed book series, "THE ART OF SUCCESS" and "PROCRASTINATION TRIUMPH," he delves into varied facets of personal and professional growth. Each series offers a unique perspective on mastering life's challenges and seizing opportunities for success. Discover more of Dilip Patil's work, available across various platforms, and continue your journey of learning and growth.

THE ART OF SUCCESS SERIES

1. [Empowering Yourself to Achieve Success](): This title empowers you to cultivate a mindset conducive to success and fulfillment. It guides you on a transformative exploration of personal development guided by core principles, actionable strategies, and inspiring anecdotes.

2. [The Path to Lasting Happiness:]() Discover the keys to enduring happiness, navigating aspects like purpose, mindset, relationships, resilience, and more. Develop communication finesse, nurture

empathy, and acquire skills for multifaceted success.

3. Yoga Flow for Tech Minds: This title harmonizes ancient wisdom with modern science to enhance productivity, reduce stress, and foster holistic well-being in the digital age. It offers practices tailored for tech minds seeking balance.

4. The Success Habits: Delve into the psychology of success to instill winning habits and unlock your full potential. Equip yourself with actionable strategies to elevate your productivity, career, and overall fulfillment.

5. The Success Mindset: Discover the secrets to attaining goals and crafting your desired reality. Learn how to nurture a winning mindset, dismantle limiting beliefs, and unleash boundless potential.

6. Endurance: Journey deep into enduring and transcending life's tests—an invaluable companion on your path of growth and adaptability.

7. The Power of Adaptability: This book complements The Success Formula by exploring adaptability's remarkable influence on shaping destinies.

8. The Success Formula: Unlock success and potential with fundamental principles, tools, and

real-life stories. This guide acts as a compass for personal and professional excellence.

9. Discover the Power of Gratitude: Explore the transformative power of gratitude in personal and professional growth.
10. There are 10 Pillars of Personal Growth: embrace resilience, Foster Connections, Cultivate Well-being, and Reach the Zenith of Success.

PROCRASTINATION TRIUMPH SERIES

1. Achieve It Now: An essential guide to overcoming procrastination and improving the future is Beat Procrastination for a Brighter Tomorrow.
2. Temporal Triumph: Defeat Procrastination, Embrace Time Mastery, and Achieve Your Destiny.
3. Action Accelerator: Practical Strategies to Eliminate Procrastination, Propel Your Life and Career Forward.
4. Pathway Pioneer: Overcome Procrastination Through Strategic Habit and Build for Lasting Growth.

LEADERSHIP TRANSFORMED

1. Leadership Awakening: Ignite Self-Awareness, Build Confidence, Foster Growth, And Embark on Your Leadership Journey

2. Visionary Pathways: Unleash Creativity, Foster Resilience, Amplify Impact, and Master Transformational Leadership
3. Masterful Communication: Enhance Influence, Improve Relationships, Boost Persuasion and Transform Leadership Skills

Each book in the series builds on the last, providing a complete arsenal for personal and professional success.

To explore these titles further and for purchasing information, please visit https://www.amazon.com/author/patildilip.

May these books help you reach your most significant potential and succeed.

With gratitude and best wishes for your continued journey,

YOUR GIFT: "THE SUCCESS FORMULA"

The Success Formula complements the principles explored in "Decision Dynamics: Navigate Complexity, Solve Problems, Cultivate Impact, and Empower Leadership through Strategy," providing actionable steps to achieving your goals and enhancing your life.

To download your free copy, click the link below or scan the QR code:

This eBook is my way of saying thank you and supporting you in your journey toward success and happiness.

www.ingramcontent.com/pod-product-compliance
Lightning Source LLC
Chambersburg PA
CBHW050058230526
45470CB00004B/1581